Landmark Visitors Guide

North Y

Bri

The Horizon Press

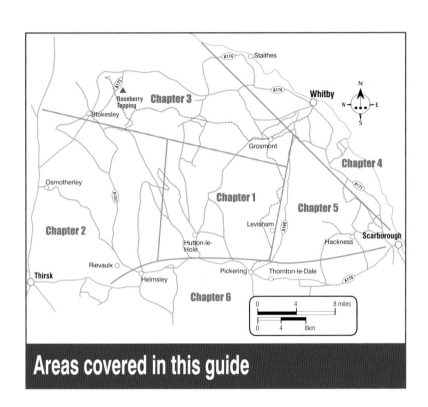

Areas covered in this guide

Opposite page: Hutton-le-Hole

2

Contents

Maps

Top Tips

Rievaulx Abbey

Tranquil ruins set in a secluded corner of Rye Dale outside the village of Helmsley.

Sutton Bank

Spectacular viewpoint over the Vale of Mowbray. National Park centre and walking trails and the White Horse of Kilburn close by.

Roseberry Topping

Mini Matterhorn near Great Ayton with extensive views over Teesside to the north and the Cleveland Hills.

Staithes

Tiny fishing harbour where Captain Cook once lived. See if you can squeeze down Dog Loup, the narrowest street in the country.

Whitby

Busy working harbour. Captain Cook Museum in the house where he boarded as an apprentice. Jet jewellery. Kipper smoking and the best fish restaurant north of Cornwall. Whitby Abbey where the date of Easter was settled dominates the town at the top of 199 steps. Dracula Museum.

Robin Hood's Bay

Loose yourself along the winding smugglers' alleys or fish for tiny crabs and other sea creatures at low tide.

Ravenscar

Visit the 'town that never was', or learn about the strange and pungent alchemy of its long-gone alum industry

Thornton-le-Dale

Pretty waterside thatch-roofed cottages

Hutton-le-Hole

Rye Dale Folk Museum of restored farm houses and shops. See if you can find how witches were kept at bay in days gone by! Choclatier works in the village

Falling Foss Tea Garden

A hidden gem tucked away in secluded woodland towards the head of Little Beck valley.

Below: Taking the flocks to the moors

Mostly administered by the North York Moors National Park Authority, this is a region of high moorland where come July a purple haze of glorious heather stretches 50 kilometres from the North Sea, to Osmotherley in the west. It is a land of contrasts, from fertile dales with hidden abbeys and unspoilt villages, to sheep pasture and grouse moors, with a wild open coastline where Captain Cook, explorer of much of the South Pacific learned his trade.

While the whole area, especially the national park, is classed as 'The Moors', and certainly much of the land remains heather covered as nature intended, geographically the countryside could not be more varied. What we expect of true heather moorland covers the central and largest part of the moors. High sweeping tracts of purple ridges separated by deeply cut green dales drain southwards into the Vale of Pickering where the rich soil was laid down in a pre-historic lake. In the south a series of flat-topped hills – the Tabular Hills, give way to an abrupt west facing escarpment where on a clear day you can see the elegant towers of York Minster. Northwards lie the Cleveland Hills where Roseberry Topping, Middlesbrough's 'Matterhorn', tests the wind of its aspiring climbers. The narrow strip of land bordering the surf battered coast marks a complete change of scenery like nowhere else and where a special kind of fishing boat was invented. Finally the south-eastern corner of the moors is mostly covered by plantations of pine forest; here you can drive or cycle, or maybe walk along a waymarked trail to one of the strange rocky outcrops such as the Bridestones, isolated weather-warn pinnacles.

People have put their mark on the landscape since the first settlers moved here around 9,000 years ago, leaving enigmatic cairns and stones that later became wayside crosses – Ralph's Cross the symbol of the North York Moors National Park Authority is one of them. Farms where the settlers made their roots have modern counterparts in the stone dwellings set amongst today's green fields. Trainee Roman soldiers studied fortress engineering, only to knock them down and start all over again. Monastic orders found tranquillity in secluded valleys or on a wind-swept cliff top until Henry VIII's agents threw them out. Riches from beneath the earth spawned new industries, from alum and jet mined on the coast, to the ironstone around Rosedale which fed the burgeoning Teesside iron and steel industry. Even now there are miners working far out under the North Sea at depths of around 5000 feet, exploiting beds of potash beneath the north-eastern corner of the moors. All this be it historical or present day, together with the need to build homes and fresh industries has to be carefully monitored and this is where national park enters into the plan of things. The statutory duty of the North York Moors National Park Authority is basically to preserve their part of the British countryside for all time. However, this does not mean that the national park is allowed to become fossilised, for like the other British national parks The Moors is a living entity where people live and earn their living, be it from the land, or providing accommodation and refreshment for visitors who come to enjoy the unique landscape.

As a holiday destination, the North York Moors has everything to offer, whether it be sight-seeing, cycling, walking, playing on the beach, or fishing, either sea, river or lake. Public transport on one of the two scenic railways crossing the moors, or hopping on or off the Moorsbus network, and the excellent local bus services makes it possible to leave the car at home.

Moors Message

Tread gently – and spare the fragile wildlife

Don't allow fires to get out of control – huge sections of the moors are regularly damaged by careless fires.

Dogs – keep them under control at all times.

Fences and Walls – it costs money to repair damaged boundaries; only cross at gates or stiles.

Weather – watch out for mist and be prepared for sudden drops of temperature.

Footpaths – are only for feet. Bicycles and horses can only be ridden on bridleways.

Take care at the coast – stay away from the unstable cliffs. Check with locals and make sure you don't get cut off by the tide

A Little Vocabulary

Beck – stream

Boggle – hobgoblin

Fret – sea mist

Gill – small steep sided valley

Griff – ravine cut by water

Howe – burial mound

Keld – spring or well

Nab – projecting part of hill

Ness – headland into the sea

Riding – former administrative area of Yorkshire – Old English for 'a third'

Rigg – ridge

Roak – mist or fog

Scar – steep rocky outcrop

Slack – shallow dell

Syke – small stream or gutter

Swang – marsh or bog

Topping – conical hill

Wyke – sheltered bay

1. The Central Moors

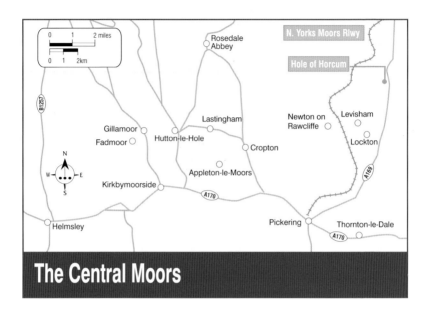

The Central Moors

Conveniently bordered by two roads one major and one not quite so busy, the central moors cover the high ground between the A169, Pickering to Whitby road in the east and the B1257, Helmsley to Stokesley road in the west. In between the land is deeply cut by four remote south draining valleys, while the moors above Esk Dale form their northern boundary. It is the latter dale which while still flooded at the end of the last Ice Age gouged its southern cousins. Each dale has its own special character and history, and therefore we can take them one at a time working slowly from east to west.

Newtondale

What better way to look at this dale or at least its tributary carved by Levisham Beck, than by stopping at the **Hole of Horcum** scenic car park beside the A169? Look out across the valley and then down to the tiny stream over 250 feet below in the valley bottom. With a natural amphitheatre at its head, surely this minute rivulet couldn't possibly have carved such a deep ravine? For the answer we must go back something like 10,000 years towards the end of the last Ice Age when, in an earlier form of global warming, ice covering the land began to melt faster than that over what became the North Sea. As a result a huge lake was formed in Esk Dale a few miles north of the Hole created by a natural dam. Unable to flow eastwards the dam eventually gave way and caused a catastrophic flood scouring the central dales, but nowhere as dramatically as in the Hole of Horcum.

In later times and up to the present, landslips have continued to widen the Hole, but in days gone by, the locals had a more imaginative answer to what made such a deep gorge. They gave credit for it to a local giant who depending on where you lived was called either Wade or Horcum. In this case it was Horcum who in a fit of temper scooped up a handful of earth and threw it at his wife, only for it to land on what became Blakey Topping a mile to the east: the strange thing is that the hillock could easily fill the Hole.

If you have a couple of hours or so to spare, there is an interesting 5 miles walk exploring the dale and moors from the car park. With it is the added attraction of the Horse Shoe Inn at Levisham about half way round, but to reach **Levisham** by car you must

The Horse Shoe Inn at Levisham makes a welcome break during a walk on the moors

drive down the Pickering road to the side turning into Lockton. Both villages have let time go by and to drive from one to the other you have to take a steep road plummeting into the valley only to rise again by a series of hairpin bends. At one time there was a thriving community surrounding the mill (now a private house), in the valley bottom; it was served along with Levisham by the tiny isolated church of St Mary. Danish sculpture in some of its ornamentation dates it from the tenth-century when the area was settled by Norsemen.

Lockton might be a sleepy place today, but in 1697 it appears to have been a hotbed of local intrigue. On a plaque tucked away on the side of a house opposite the youth hostel, are the names of eight benefactors who paid for a village well to be dug. Fine as it went, but what later quarrel led to one of the names being removed? There is no pub in the village, but the Fox and Rabbit a onetime farmhouse inn a little way down the main road towards Pickering also has a children's play area.

Like many of the central dales, there is no significant road or village along Newtondale, but the narrow valley does play host to the North York Moors Railway from Grosmont to Pickering. Moorland to the west of the dale is given over to the plantations of Cropton Forest where it is possible to wander along forest walks served by the railway. Another place to visit on foot is the romantic ruin of **Skelton Tower** – there is a short footpath from Levisham by way of Dundale Pond, itself a rarity of standing water on the dry moors. It was designed as a shooting lodge in 1850 by the Reverend Skelton vicar of Levisham; allegedly he

built it so he could write his sermons in peace, but if local folklore is correct, it was also somewhere for him to enjoy a quiet drink away from prying eyes! Levisham has its own halt at the bottom of yet another steep road, but to reach the far side of the dale by road it will be necessary to drive into Pickering, and then out by way of the linear village of **Newton-on-Rawcliffe** (pub and caravan site), a torturous route in order to climb out of Newtondale. The village whose layout was dictated by a line of springs on the normally dry surrounding limestone countryside is, as they say, well worth a visit.

By following the minor road signposted to Cawthorne and with a keen-eyed navigator sitting next to you, you will eventually come to a lay-by with a signpost saying '**To the Roman Practice Works'**. Even now after almost two thousand years, it is still possible to trace the outlines of at least three earthworks. Along with the usual oblong or square formatted camps, some are irregular or even semi-circular in shape, or with deep man-trapping twin ditches. All this has lead to a theory that it was a training depot for Roman military engineers, a theory further enhanced by the fact that some earthworks overlap earlier schemes. The camps were linked by a road from Malton over to the coast near Whitby: there is a well preserved section of Roman Road above Wheeldale named after Wade, our friend Horcum's alter-ego.

Several cycle routes run through Cropton Forest and a winding moor land road through the forest beyond Newton-on-Rawcliffe follows the Roman Road for part of the way to Goathland and the Esk Valley. **Cropton** the forest's namesake village has its own brewery at the back of a pub which has been selling real ale since at least 1613. It names its ales after local features, such as a stout which commemorates the 18th century arctic explorer and inventor of the crow's nest, William Scoresby who was born in the village. A little to the northwest of Cropton are the remains of a Norman earth bank and timber palisaded castle built by Robert de Stuteville to protect trade routes across the moors. Despite its age, the remains of its protective banks and ditches are still quite visible.

Rosedale

Beyond Cropton, a side road drops steeply into **Rosedale.** A narrow winding by-road follows the dale, but rather than simply drive along the dale, why not take the link road to Farndale, if only for a little way? The reason for this diversion is that it leads to the picturesque village of **Lastingham** where the stone crypt is venerated as the sole remnant of a Celtic monastery founded in 659 by the 'Four Cs', Cedd, Chad, Celin and Cynebal. Nothing is left of the timber and turf-roofed original the which Danes destroyed in the 9th century, but King William I, the Conqueror, restored it in 1078, only for the monks to abruptly leave and set up a rival monastery in York. A later church built over the crypt is an attraction in itself, but the readily accessible crypt remains one of the most impressive pieces of Norman architecture in England. The Blacksmith's Arms opposite the church has a curious history; in 1806 it was run by a Mrs Carter wife of the curate and in order to feed their 13 children on a stipend of £20 a year, the vicar eked out his income by fishing while his wife ran the pub. The excuse he gave to his archdeacon was that he was only following Christ's teaching by feeding the

Lastingham Church crypt dates from 659

13

The Blacksmith's Arms opposite Lastingham Church was run by the vicar's wife in 1806

local equivalent of the 5,000, many of whom had to travel a long way to reach his church. What the archdeacon had to say about this was not recorded, but the Carters kept their pub and church for many more years.

Before exploring Rosedale there is yet another diversion away from Lastingham. This time southwards through its neighbour **Spaunton** where the Manorial Court Leet, a civil court dating back to the Middle Ages still meets once a year to settle things like boundary disputes. A couple of miles further on is **Appleton-le-Moors,** a planned village built eight centuries before the need for overspill towns. Laid out as a linear development, the wide main street allows each tenant

access to common grazing, and the houses, or tofts have road access back and front. Its medieval pattern is still evident in the shape of the long, narrow strip fields, easily the most uniquely preserved layout anywhere in the national park. Appleton Hall, the school-house and village church were all built around 1860 by the architect, JL Pearson.

Returning to Rosedale, there is a choice of two roads; either along the tree-shaded valley bottom from Crofton, or by a high level moorland road starting from where the Lastingham road drops down to Hutton-le-Hole. This road crosses Spaunton Moor before dropping in a heart-wrenching descent to **Rosedale Abbey**, the dale's one and

Above:The masonry on the right of the picture is all that is left of Rosedale Abbey

Right: Curious offerings are often left on White Cross otherwise known as Fat Betty

Below: The Lion, better known as the Blakey Inn, claims to be 'the pub on the top of the world'.

only settlement of any significance. A valley of green sheep pasture in spring, then brown and orange as the bracken dies in autumn, the dale has regained the tranquility it once lost when the high ground was mined for ironstone, and Rosedale's abbey watched over this land across the centuries. The religious house which gave the village its name was a small Cistercian nunnery or priory, founded in the 12th century with a community of nine nuns and a prioress, but as with most ecclesiastical houses the abbey was closed in 1535; the nuns dispersed and the stones used to build the village church. The only remaining trace of the priory is a tower-like structure in the church yard, and the motto *'Omnia Vanitas',* [All is Vanity] on the lintel over the north door. There are a couple of cosy pubs and an excellent tea room in the village which is also a good centre for walks on the surrounding moorland ridges, or 'riggs' in the old Norse as they are known hereabouts.

Take the steep road to the north west out of the dale (the valley road is the only comparatively level road and even that has its ups and downs), then climb with it out on to heather covered Rosedale Moor, past pre-historic burial mounds, but don't confuse them with the more numerous hummocks made by medieval coal miners. Bearing left with the road as it turns the valley head, you will see on your right, one of the crosses, or standing stones that marked ancient routes across the moors – both the Coast-to-Coast Walk and the Lyke Wake Walk pass this way along tracks created over a thousand years ago. This one in particular is officially called White Cross, but is better known by locals as Fat Betty and is

something of an enigma. In structure it is a squat upright pillar topped by a circular white-painted stone rather like a grinding wheel. At one time the 'wheel' used to be free and people left gifts beneath it for other travellers or even local deities, but due to it being knocked off its base by less caring wanderers, it is now firmly cemented to the main upright. The practice of leaving gifts continues, but now it is food and drink as well as money which are left along with on occasions, certain items of intimate ladies' underwear! Answer that if you can!

Where the moorland road makes its final turn on the valley head, a hundred yards down the side road on your right is Ralph's Cross, the symbol of the North York Moors National Park. Technically known as 'Young Ralph', ('Old Ralph' is a smaller cross, about 200 yards to the west), it stands at the junction of the roads to Westerdale, Rosedale, Castleton and Hutton-le-Hole and was erected as legend has it, by a farmer who found a traveller who had died from exhaustion.

A little over a mile down the Hutton-le-Hole road, the Lion Inn which is known better as Blakey Inn, has offered sustenance to travellers since the 1500s. This was when monks belonging to the Order of Crouched Friars from Guisborough Priory set up the first refuge. Standing at 1325 feet above sea level and claiming to be the 'pub on the top of the world', in its time it has been a monastic hospital, a market and a bunk house for ironstone miners. It was a wild lawless place at one time especially when cock fighting took place in the hollowed top of a pre-historic burial mound on the moor above the inn.

Riches from beneath the Moors – part 1

Ironstone mining

During the Jurassic period when dinosaurs roamed the land, ironstone was laid down in a part shallow sea, part swamp covering much of what is now the North York Moors. Prompted by the monks of Guisborough Priory, the stone was mined to make iron for everyday tools, dug from simple open pits and quarries around Rosedale Moor. When the Industrial Revolution got under way in the mid-1800s, large scale mining completely altered the face of the dale. Roughly following a line along the 690 foot contour, mines both open cast and underground exploited the natural resource. In its mined form, ironstone is full of impurities and has to be fired, or calcined, in order to release the metallic content. This operation was carried out in coal-fired kilns which although derelict since the 1920s can still be seen along the dale sides. The resulting ore was transported to the Teesside iron and steel industry along a railway that first contoured round both sides of the dale, over the head of Farndale to Bloworth Crossing and then down to the mainline at Battersby Junction below the Cleveland Hills. From Bloworth Crossing wagons made the steep descent on a cable operated by a stationery engine. Illicit passengers sometimes rode the trucks as an easy way to reach the shops until a runaway caused by a broken cable led to a serious accident.

Ironstone kilns, Rosedale Moor

*Ralph Cross, the
enigmatic symbol of
the North York Moors*

Farndale daffodils are a delight every spring

Hutton-le-Hole

Bloworth Crossing is an important highlight for long distance walkers who part company there; some to continue north along the Cleveland Way, or others descending into Esk Dale for the Coast to Coast: only Lyke Wake walkers continue a little further along the old railway track on their way to Ravenscar.

Farndale

If the Lakeland poet William Wordsworth had had cause to visit Farndale one spring, the odds are that when wandering lonely as a cloud, the host of golden daffodils he spied might have been those in Farndale rather than Ullswater. The dale's wild daffodils are a sight to be seen each spring when a special Daffodil Walk links the two Farndale hamlets of Church Houses and Low Mill. Driving down into the dale from Blakey Ridge is tricky at the best of times – there are not that many roads given the accolade of five arrows by the Ordnance Survey, indicating a gradient constantly steeper than 1 in 5: coming from Hutton-le-Hole at the lower end of the valley is not much easier, with its narrow width and tight bends, especially if the roads are busy. The best way to explore Rosedale therefore, is to use the Moorsbus service at all times, but essentially at daffodil time. Cyclists on the other hand can revel in the enjoyment of riding round the twin crests of the dale, up Blakey Ridge from Hutton-le-Hole and back on the almost arrow-straight track along the crest of Rudland Rigg from Bloworth Crossing.

The main and really the only village in Rosedale is **Hutton-le-Hole**, a village the Victorians spoke of as 'unplanned and untidy', and where drunkenness and cock-fighting were an every day affair. Go there now and you will see how our ideas of what is attractive have gone several steps forward since then; its spacious open unplanned layout of scattered groups of cottages around a green that slopes to its 'beck' is the one thing above all others that draws people back time and again. In fairness to our Victorian forebears, it should be pointed out that in their day Hutton-le-Hole held regular fairs and cattle shows which no doubt gave the ironstone miners who lodged there an excuse to let their hair down.

People have lived in and around Hutton-le-Hole since the Bronze Age as witness what the OS map calls, in Gothic letters, 'pillow mounds', a mysterious group of grassed-over cairns to the north-west of the village. The land had long been under cultivation when William the Conqueror's scribes recorded in the Domesday Book the equivalent of over 1000 acres of farm land connected to the village. Much of the link with a time gone by can be seen at the **Ryedale Folk Museum** in the middle of the village. With the freedom of being able to wander around restored buildings, all of which have been brought in from the surrounding moors, you can step back in time to the 17th, 18th and 19th centuries or even earlier. Thatched cottages, a cruck-framed 16th century manor house, kitchen gardens, flower meadows, an Edwardian photographic studio, old shops and craftsmen's workshops give a hint of what life was like in previous centuries. There is also a reconstructed

Iron Age roundhouse, and rare breed farm animals very much like the stock reared by the ancients, roam in paddocks close by.

The museum hosts a programme of special events ranging from concerts in the Manor House to seasonal celebrations, folk festivals and archaeological events catering for the old and young. Along with attractions linked to the museum, Hutton-le-Hole has a wide range of craft workshops scattered around the village, together with the Chocolate Factory (but no Charlie, although you can watch the chocolatiers in action), an inn and a small tea room to satisfy the inner man and woman after a tiring, yet enjoyable look back in time.

Witches, Hobs & the Hand of Glory

While you are exploring Ryedale Folk Museum, make sure you go into one of the farm houses and while there take a careful look at the supporting timbers around the fireplace. Near the top of the left-hand (as facing), upright you will see a strange geometric pattern. This is a witch post designed to prevent witches entering the house and a few can still be found in the old farmhouses throughout the moors.

Witches were once common on the moors

Hobs lived up on the moors, or deep inside secluded wooded valleys. Friendly chaps unless you crossed them, they would help by churning butter during the night, or do other tasks without being asked, but woe-betide anyone who didn't leave them a midnight snack, for chaos would then reign.

The Hand of Glory is a macabre link with crueller times. When a man was hanged from a gibbet out on the moors, it was considered good luck by thieves to cut off one of his hands and use it to mesmerise potential victims by setting a candle made from human fat between the fingers. One of these hands is in Pannet Park Museum at Whitby; blackened with age it still gives a shudder to everyone who sees it.

Above: Restored grocer's shop, Ryedale Folk Museum

Above: Ryedale Folk Museum, Hutton-le-Hole

A blacksmith shows his skill, Ryedale Folk Museum

Bransdale, Sleightholme Dale and Kirkdale

Strictly speaking these are one dale carved by Hodge Beck as it runs south through the Tabular Hills, but due to a couple of very tight sections in its middle reaches, the dale is quite definitely in three sections. At the top of the dale is Bransdale a perfect gem waiting to be discovered by all who take the trouble to explore its seclusion. There is no actual village, or in fact, a motor road out of the dale, but the scattered groups of old farmhouses, a mill and a shooting lodge are a link with gentler days gone by.

The dale makes its first narrowing by emerging as wooded Sleightholme Dale. Here the beck makes its final cut through the Tabular Hills into Kirkdale, before meandering out onto the Vale of Pickering's floodplain.

While the uppermost part of the dale is simply one of exquisite unspoilt meadows and moorland scenery, it does have one extra-special man made feature; Bransdale Mill restored by National Trust Acorn working parties is now run as a centre for education and conservation, but it dates mostly from the early 1800s, although built on much older foundations.

The term **Tabular Hills** incidentally refers to the flat-topped limestone hills. They mark the southern escarpment of the moors between Rosedale and the Hambleton Hills near the western moors escarpment. The hills were created by ice lying relatively still on the highest land, but moving more rapidly along the valleys. Using water brought by a complex of channels from out on the high moors in 1747, local landowner Joseph Foord helped the twin villages of **Fadmoor and Gillamoor** develop; each is endowed with a pub selling good food and drink and where the temptation to tarry is great, but one cannot be criticised for having the occasional peek at the attractive cottage gardens of both villages. The former is a pretty collection of stone built houses set around a village green, and Gillamoor is best known for its 'Surprise View' over Farndale.

Right at the bottom of Kirkdale and giving the dale its title, the venerable Saxon church of St **Gregory's Minster** stands almost completely surrounded by woodland and isolated from any village. The main structural link with its Saxon founders is the narrow arch between the nave and the tower, but it is the sundial above the south doorway which takes us back into centuries past. In a form of runic lettering used by the Vikings, a sundial dating from 1060, states that:

'Orm, the son of Gamal, bought St Gregoriuos Minster when it was all broken and fallen, and he has made it new. In the days of Edward the King and Tosti the Earl'.

Riccal Dale, Ash Dale & Beck Dale

These final and most westerly dales in the Central Moors are the shortest; none has a motor road, but there is a marvellous high level partly unfenced way climbing from Helmsley by way of the farming hamlet of Carlton right over to the upper reaches of Bransdale. Being relatively traffic-free it makes an ideal day-long cycle run; there are plenty of unofficial picnic sites, and of course, there are lots of woodland walks along rights of way in the forested depths of the dales.

Places to Visit

Ryedale Folk Museum w

Hutton-le-Hole ☎ (01751) 417367
Open all year daily from 10:00 am 5:30pm. From 28 October to mid March 10:00am – dusk. Closed early December to mid January. Dogs welcome on leads.

Hutton-le-Hole Chocolate Factory w

Hutton-le-Hole YO62 6UA
w: www.the-chocolate-factory. co.uk
Open: 10:30am-5:00pm, March 1st - October 31st. Tuesday – Sunday (open Bank Holiday Mondays)

Ironstone Mining Remains

It is possible to trace the surface remnants of this one-time major industry, especially by following the dale-edge railway and processing kilns.

Pre-Norman churches

St Gregory's Minster w

Kirkdale
See the Saxon sundial and south doorway of this hidden gem

St Cedd's Church w

Lastingham
Explore the ancient crypt dating from 659

Water Mills

There are surviving mills in Bransdale, Farndale, Newtondale and Rye Dale, but most have been converted to private houses.

Moorland Crosses

See: Young, Ralph and Old Ralph and White Cross (Fat Betty) adjacent to the road above Rosedale.

Roman Practice Camps

Waymarked path (leaflet available from tourist offices), in Cawthorne Forest between Cropton and Newton-on-Rawcliffe. (GR785 902)

Daffodils

Use the Moorsbus to visit the famous Farndale daffodils in spring, or stroll through the meadows at other times.

Recommended Walking Areas Suitable For Families

Hole of Horcum to Levisham Moor Skelton Tower can be reached from Levisham.
Farndale Daffodil Walk – from Church Houses to Low Mill Rosedale Ironstone Railway Track. Circular walks of varying distances can be made by using the level track-bed of the abandoned track.

Rosedale Abbey village also makes an ideal base for both valley and high level walks on the surrounding moors.
Forest walks in Cropton Forest from the North Yorkshire Moors Railway, or from picnic sites reached by forest road.
The circular walk from Hutton-le-Hole to Lastingham and back will link two unspoilt villages each with an interesting history.

Off Road Cycling Areas

Tracks in Cropton Forest offer scope for everyone from gentle rides to the hardest courses.
The moor road north by way of Carlton from Helmsley to the head of Bransdale and back by way of Rudland Rigg or Farndale should make a pleasant day's ride. Alternatively ride up Rudland Rigg from Hutton-le-Hole to Bloworth Crossing and come back along the ironstone railway to Rosedale Abbey.

Horse Riding

There are bridleways into Farndale from Hutton-le-Hole, or along Rudland Rigg and in Newtondale where there is a dedicated horse trail.

2. BILSDALE, THE HAMBLETON & CLEVELAND HILLS AND THE WESTERN ESCARPMENT

Bilsdale marks the boundary between the high central moors and the western escarpment. In contrast to the central moors, the rivers Seph and Rye have carved deep into the landscape, but unlike the moorland rivers, their valleys are more suited to arable farming, where the gentle landscape attracted monks of old to build their monasteries. The Hambleton and Cleveland hills also provided safe routes for drovers slowly moving their cattle and sheep towards southern markets. Where the A170 climbs steadily out of Helmsley it marks the boundary between underlying shales and gritstones to its north and chalky limestone to the south. All end abruptly in the west with a dramatic escarpment falling steeply into the Vale of Mowbray.

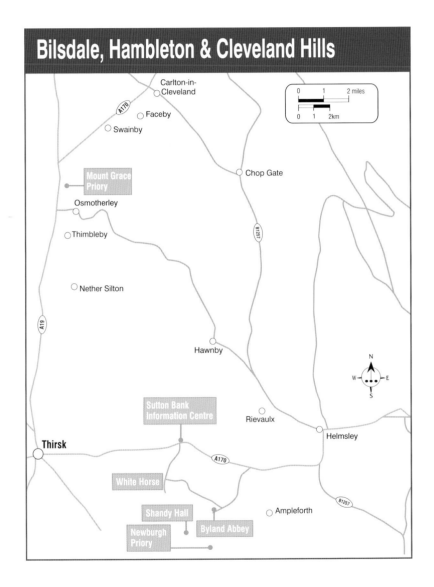

Bilsdale, Hambleton & Cleveland Hills

Carlton-in-Cleveland

Faceby

Swainby

A170

Mount Grace Priory

Osmotherley

Thimbleby

Chop Gate

B1257

Nether Silton

A19

Hawnby

Sutton Bank Information Centre

Rievaulx

Helmsley

Thirsk

A170

White Horse

Shandy Hall

Amplefoth

Byland Abbey

B1257

Newburgh Priory

N
W   E
S

0   1   2 miles
0   1   2km

Bilsdale is part of wide meandering Rye Dale, but in its upper reaches Bilsdale together with its own tributary Raisdale, cuts deeply into the Cleveland Hills. Erosion begun by glacial action has created a switchback of steep-sided hills, outliers as well as within the complex moorland landscape. If you drive up the B1257 from the general direction of Middlesbrough and having left Great Broughton behind, climb through woodland, first up Clay Bank, then Hasty Bank where the road crosses the watershed, the first settlement has the strange title of **Chop Gate**: the name has nothing to do with a woodsman and his axe, but has links with a time when essential goods were traded by itinerant carriers. Pronounced locally as 'Chop Yat', 'Chop' comes from the Old Norse word 'ceap' or 'kaup' for a bagman, or peddler; 'Yat' or 'Gate' is a form of 'gata' which again is Old Norse, meaning a street or road, – the way by which peddlers came into Bilsdale.

Passing farmsteads and hamlets on its way south, in four miles the road reaches a cruck-framed thatched building known as **Spout House** – a crucked building is one which is supported by a pair of curved timbers extending from the floor to the roof. Until it closed in 1914 in favour of the adjacent Sun Inn, Spout House was the local hostellery and a stopping place along the valley road. Originally a farmworker's cottage built in 1550; Spout House became an inn in 1714, but was abandoned when the new pub was opened across the yard. In 1982 it was saved by the North York Moors National Park Authority who brought it back to its former glory, but sadly the bar remains closed.

Spout House and the Breach of Copyright Trial

In 1895 a local artist Ralph Headley painted a group of local huntsmen enjoying a convivial drink inside the bar parlour of Spout House. A member of Bovril's advertising department who didn't know the law of Breach of Copyright too well commissioned a version of the painting showing the huntsmen drinking, not whisky, but Bovril. As a result the incensed artist was able to sue and won considerable damages.

A little further along the dale a side road westwards above the infant River Rye leads to **Hawnby** – its pub, the Hawnby Hotel is one of those little hideaways where time is counted not by years, but in decades. The road ever narrowing, leads on towards the upper dale, through woodland and out on to the open moors. There is a woodland picnic site at the bottom of a steep dip above Hawnby, effectively at the road's end near Low Cote – (no pub, so take a picnic). If you enjoy off the beaten track walking, then any of the dozens of paths around the upper Rye are a delight.

The Hambleton Hills

Starting in Cumbria and after wandering around various sites in the north of England for eight years, in 1143 Cistercian monks built a small abbey at **Old Byland,** but even then they couldn't settle and it took another thirty years by way of a temporary abode at Stocking before they eventually settled. There is a lovely drive around upper Rye Dale, especially if you are not in a hurry; it twists and turns before climbing out onto the side of the Hambleton Hills to reach Old Byland. If you look around the church you will find many early Norman fragments, possibly from the Cistercians' temporary abode. Less than two miles as the crow flies across the gorge-like depths of Flassen Dale, but a lot more by road, is **Scawton,** one of the finest examples of a preserved medieval English village.

A narrow side turning off the main road a couple of miles outside Helmsley drops into the valley where, even if you are expecting it, the view of Rievaulx Abbey simply takes your breath away. Not only that, but to guild the lily so to speak, Rievaulx Terrace completes the idyllic scene.

Rievaulx Abbey & the Terrace

In 1132 St Bernard of Clairvaux decided to build an abbey on this a perfect spot. With just 12 followers the simple retreat became one of the wealthiest monasteries in medieval England, the first northern Cistercian monastery whose majestic mellow limestone walls and pillars are the jewel in the crown of the North York Moors.

Although the Cistercian monks were attracted to Rievaulx by its tranquil seclusion, they were not content to simply hide themselves away; much of the rich agricultural land throughout Rye Dale and the Hambleton Hills is partly due to their efforts. By developing grange farms, the monks honed skills in animal husbandry and also taught themselves iron smelting.

St Aeldred, the third abbot of Rievaulx, summed everything about the abbey by saying; 'Everywhere peace, everywhere serenity, and a marvellous freedom from the tumult of the world'. He was venerated during his lifetime as a wise preacher: canonised after his death in 1167, the flow of pilgrims continued to arrive at his tomb until the abbey's dissolution in 1588. King Henry VIII gave it and its lands to Thomas Manners, first Earl of Rutland who set about its systematic destruction, but fortunately seemed to have lost interest along the way, leaving behind a monastic ruin, 'free from the tumult of the world'.

Rievaulx Terrace

As the National Trust handbook says, 'this is one of Ryedale's true gems'. The terrace was built as a pleasure ground in 1758 by Thomas Duncombe for family picnics. Two temples, one Ionic and the other Tuscan stand at either end of a grassy terrace amidst flower-filled woodland where careful tree felling has opened views of the abbey.

Rievaulx Abbey from The Terrace

Ionic Temple, Rievaulx Terrace

Helmsley

Although there is more about **Helmsley** in Chapter 6, we must at least give it passing mention while continuing our tour of the western moors. The old town is set around a spacious market square with houses backing on to the River Rye. With a castle, a walled garden and Duncombe Park nearby, it makes an ideal stopping place, especially when looking for refreshment in one of the restaurants and cafes lining the marketplace.

The A170 following the southern foot of the moors makes a dog-leg to avoid the Rye's floodplain, and then climbs across the forested expanse of Scawton Moor to reach Sutton Bank.

Where this road turns west at Sproxton, dire warnings prevent caravan-towing drivers from attempting the descent of Sutton Bank. For them, and us for the alternative is a much pleasanter route, along the tree-girthed foot of the moors, outliers of the Hambleton Hills. The by-road winds its way through a series of sleepy villages; first is **Ampleforth** where a Benedictine monastery founded by Father Bolton in 1802, developed as a famous public school. Ampleforth abbey church designed by Gilbert Scott is open to visitors, as is the orchard whose apples are turned into an excellent apple brandy as good as anything from Normandy. The nearby

Byland Abbey

village is one of simple rural charm and has two interesting pubs where you can sample the abbey's apple brandy.

Approaching **Byland Abbey**, its major glory stands out from the road. Even though only half of the once massive rose window remains since the Dissolution, it is easy to imagine its magnificence: this is the abbey the monks from Cumbria spent so long in finding. As well as the rose window you can find sections of mosaic tiled floors, while outside there are traces of fish ponds where the monks bred carp for their Friday meals.

Monks were not always as saintly as we think

During the middle ages the monks of Byland and Rievaulx disputed ownership of land in Rye Dale. As a result channels below Helmsley are the result of engineering work carried out in a bad tempered attempt to divert the river.

A mile south of the national park boundary, **Newburgh Priory**, now a country mansion, was built by Augustinian Canons in 1150. A macabre story has it that the body of Oliver Cromwell is buried there: after he was ignominiously exhumed from Westminster Abbey and beheaded at Tyburn. The body, so the story goes, was spirited away by Cromwell's daughter Mary, up to Newburgh. True or not the priory owners will not allow his supposed tomb to be opened.

A country lane beyond the priory leads back into the national park, where the stone-built cottages of **Coxwold** date from the 17th century. They line wide grassy verges leading towards the octagonal tower of the 15th century church, and then half way along the street the Faucenberg Arms commemorates the original owners of the village. At the top of the rise, almost opposite the church, is **Shandy Hall** where Laurence Sterne lived from 1760 until his death in 1768. Spending his last years as Vicar of Coxwold, he is best remembered as the author of *Tristram Shandy*. Two centuries ahead of his time, his novel is a mixture of hilariously ribald mishaps and digressions which still delight its modern readers.

Drive on for another two miles and piles of timber at the road side announce that this is **Kilburn**, where Robert Thompson better known as the Mouseman, plied his trade. A skilled craftsman, his ecclesiastical and domestic oak furniture always bore the distinctive 'signature' of a tiny church mouse, hidden somewhere only the ultimate owner could know; examples can be found in Westminster Abbey, Ampleforth and even on the Archbishop's throne in York Minster. Since his death his descendants have carried on his skills with each carver using a different symbol ranging from a lizard to a, short lived, gnome! A letter from Australia addressed with nothing other than a drawing of a mouse and the words 'Woodcarver, England', found its way to Kilburn.

The mouse which adorns all Thompson furniture

Kilburn's White Horse

A narrow lane beyond Kilburn leads towards **Kilburn White Horse**. Uniquely it is the only hill carving in the north of England, but even so cannot in all honesty be classed alongside those carved in pre-history. Visible from the A1 and the Edinburgh to London mainline, this is the work of a village schoolmaster who, in 1857 set his pupils to work carving the 314 ft long, 228 ft tall 'horse' into the chalk hillside. There is a scenic car park and picnic site beneath the horse's 'hooves' and a footpath from Sutton Bank National Park Centre, but the best way to appreciate the carving is from the road.

Yorkshire Gliding Club has an airfield above the White Horse at Roulston Scar, and you should be able to watch the graceful flight of gliders if you follow the waymarked path from the top of Sutton Bank.

Rising between wooded slopes around the White Horse and the gliding club, the rocky outcrop of **Roulston Scar** is all that remains of ancient coral reef from a tropical sea where dinosaurs roamed. Iron Age people built a massive hillfort on top of the Scar, the largest in Northern England; you can still see the defensive ditches, some are still eight feet high, but take care and watch out for gliders. A track below the Scar known locally as the 'Thief's Highway', is supposed to have been the escape route of highwaymen who plundered travellers on the Hambleton Road.

Right: The National Park Tree of Life, Sutton Bank Information Centre

Above: Kilburn White Horse

Below: View over the Vale of Mowbray from Sutton Bank

Drove Roads

Long before the coming of more efficient transport, cattle, sheep and packhorses used the high open ground to reach lowland markets. Salted fish also made its way from the coast along paved trackways which can still be traced, but the busiest traffic was the movement of animals along the western escarpment. Known as Hambleton Drove Road, it follows the escarpment from Osmotherley to Byland and onwards to Malton and York. From standing stones and cairns marking the way, the drove road was obviously old long before it became mentioned as *Regalis Via,* the 'King's Way' in medieval documents.

Drovers were hardy Scotsmen who walked cattle from as far away as the Outer Isles; little remains of their passing apart from the name 'Scotch Corner' which like its more illustrious namesake on the A1 was one of their resting places. There were also simple inns such as above Osmotherley, now only a heap of stones hiding in the heather.

Horse drawn carriages used the Hambleton Drove as a comparatively dry route. Unfortunately this particular highway has a steep descent from Black Hambleton into Osmotherley, causing one 18th century traveller to vow never to use it again. During recent times, the Hambleton Drove Road suffered from over use by 4x4 drivers and trail bikes, but a Traffic Control Order means the road is again only used by walkers, cyclists and horse riders.

Tucked away in woodland beside the A170, **Sutton Bank Information Centre** makes an ideal place to stop and learn about the national park – and there is also a tea room to please the most discerning traveller. Several waymarked walks start from it, or you could simply walk through the trees and admire the view west across the Vale of Mowbray towards the Yorkshire Dales.

About a quarter of a mile north along the edge, a side path drops towards **Gormire Lake,** the largest natural free-standing water in the moors. When the ice sheet in the vale retreated, it left behind a large block of ice surrounded by glacial debris which eventually made the lake. Native woodland of birch and oak provides an ideal habitat for a wide variety of birds and insects, together with a profusion of spring flowers. The lake doesn't seem to have a visible outflow; no doubt it soaks away into the chalky sub-soil, but at one time the locals thought it bottomless. A legend tells of a duck which managed to find an underground channel reappeared in Kirkbymoorside, 13 miles/21km away! The Ordnance Survey map of the area indicates *'Fairies Parlour (Cave)'*, a little way along the edge from where the path drops to the lake. Unfortunately fairies have never been seen in recent years, neither is there much of a cave, but children enjoy searching for it.

There is a modern course at Thirsk, but horse racing took place along the Hambleton Hills, from Sutton Bank to Hesketh Dyke from Viking times (the word 'Hesketh' comes from the Old Norse for horse racing) until the reign of Queen Anne, but all that is left are modern training gallops near Dialstone Farm where a stone dial marks the start of the onetime racecourse.

The Cleveland Way long distance trail follows the escarpment northwards, barely losing more than a few feet at a time, crossing the top of the precipitous top of Smeck Yate Bank. Below and linked by a winding byways, a scattering of tiny villages cry out to be explored. For example, in a field behind the church at **Nether Silton** a curious stone pillar with an enigmatic rhyme which has baffled people for years, stands on the site of an old manor house. There is another mystery near of the scattered hamlet of **Thimbleby,** where records speak of a Benedictine priory that suddenly vanished in 1349, possibly due to an outbreak of the Black Death; nothing is left apart from a private property called Nun House.

Osmotherley is the largest village along this part of the moors and it stands at the foot of outliers of the Cleveland Hills. The village is a sturdy grouping of stone houses and hospitable pubs: one of them proudly bears the name of 'Queen Catherine', Henry VIII's wronged wife. This is the only pub in the country to still carry her name; there were once scores up and down the land, but they changed to 'Elephant and Castle', in mockery of her title as the Infanta of Castille. Here is a village which prides itself on tidiness, the public toilet is kept fastidiously clean by a group of volunteers and visitors are moved to send fan mail and even Christmas cards!

John Wesley preached at Osmotherley and the Methodist chapel is one of the oldest in England, but even older is the market cross, as is St Stephen's church where the remains of Saxon crosses and hog's back gravestones indicate its age. Osmotherley Games shatter the peaceful scene in July with such crazy goings on as piano smashing and sheaf tossing. In quieter vein, Cod Beck Reservoir above the village has a scenic car park and picnic site, making it an ideal base for short walks exploring the surrounding moors. You can reach it from Swainby by way of Scarth Nick.

Osmotherley as a long distance walker's base

Three long distance routes meet at Osmotherley; one of them **The Lyke Wake Walk** actually starts there and following ancient 'corpse roads', reaches the North Sea at Ravenscar. There is a club to which anyone who completes the walk can join, which holds an annual wake at the Queen Catherine where members sing the traditional funeral dirge:

This yah neet, this yah neet,

Ivery neet an' all,

Fire and Fleet an' cannel leet

An' Christ tak up thi saul.

The 108 mile long **Cleveland Way** national trail comes through Osmotherley on its way from Helmsley to Filey Brigg on the North Sea coast. Following high ground most of the way it uses old tracks along the western escarpment before moving over to the coast by way of the Cleveland Hills, where it turns south at Saltburn to reach its final destination.

A 190 mile walk devised by the late A Wainwright of Lakeland guidebook fame, and known as the **Coast to Coast Walk which** joins the Irish and North Seas by way of three national parks, the Lake District, the Yorkshire Dales and the North York Moors, also passes through Osmotherley.

A mile or so below Osmotherley, 14th century **Mount Grace Priory** is set in a sheltered spot at the foot of a wooded hillside, the best preserved of only ten Carthusian Priories in England. It was here that 15 Carthusian monks lived in specially constructed independent cells, spending their days scribing illuminated manuscripts, or in prayer. Whilst living in solitary confinement, the monks were still comparatively comfortable, if a restored cell is anything to go by. Each 22ft/7.3m square two-storied cell had a fireplace and a bedroom as well as workspace. Outside there was a small herb garden and a privy kept clean by running water. Meals were served by way of an angled hole so that the monk could not see who brought it.

Close to the priory and beside the A172, the **Cleveland Tontine Inn** is named after the strange custom whereby a group of people jointly owned the property. Dating from Renaissance Italy, no single member of a tontine could claim the property, but at their death left his or her share to the others until the last inherited everything; in this case it was a local coal mine owner Brian Cooper Abbs.

Moving east along the foot of the Cleveland Hills, the national park boundary at first follows the A172, by-passing a line of attractive villages.

Above: Each monk had a small garden where he grew medicinal herbs

Right: Entrance to Monk's Cell, Mount Grace

The first going east, is **Swainby** which despite initial appearances is not a modern village, but dates from at least the 14th century. Originally it was actually a mile further east at what is now **Whorlton,** but during one of the many plagues in the Middle Ages, survivors moved just far enough to the west as to avoid the disease. A motte and bailey castle set between the two villages guarded the way on to the moors, and both places expanded rapidly during the 19th century iron-stone boom. In Whorlton church, Nicholas de Meynall whose family once owned the castle is commemorated by an effigy in bog oak dating from the 14th century. It was in Whorlton Castle that the plot to marry Mary Queen of Scots to Lord Darnley was made, but all that is left is the sturdy gatehouse bearing the coats of arms of the Meynells, Darcys and Greys.

The quiet three mile side valley of Scugdale Beck climbs to the moors by way of the of **Heathwaite, or Huthwaite** depending on which road sign you accept. Quiet though it is today, it was once the home of two remarkable people. The first was Elizabeth Harland who died in 1812 at the grand old age of 105 and the other was Henry Cooper, a giant of a man; in 1890 he was 8ft 6inches tall, and the world's tallest living man, spending his younger days as a farm labourer before joining Barnum and Bailey's Circus where he was exhibited as something of a freak. He died aged 32.

Despite its name, **Carlton in Cleveland** is in North Yorkshire, a few miles from Stokesley and just inside the national park boundary. Along with its neighbour, **Faceby,** where after weddings the groom and best man throw coins to waiting children, the village sits comfortably at the foot of hills where long distance walkers cross Carlton Bank and, if they have the time and energy, attempt to scramble on the outcrop of rocks known as the **Wainstones.** More likely they will take the excuse of stopping to admire the view north over the Cleveland plain, or watch gliders from the nearby airfield beyond Great Bonny Cliff. Alum was mined as shale from around 1600 to 1880, but little remains apart from the pretty stream, Alum Beck, which flows through **Faceby,** where the church has had a turbulent history. In the late 1800s when the new vicar,

George Sangar took over he found it almost derelict and selflessly began its restoration, not only raising the cash, but by acting as a labourer. No sooner was the church completed than it was destroyed by fire and Sangar spuriously charged with arson.

There is a switch-back moorland road up Carlton Bank to Cringle Moor where a scenic car park takes all the effort out of reaching any number of short walks along the breezy escarpment. Beyond it the road swings down into Raisdale and on to Chop Gate, where a conveniently situated pub completes this tour of the western moors and edges.

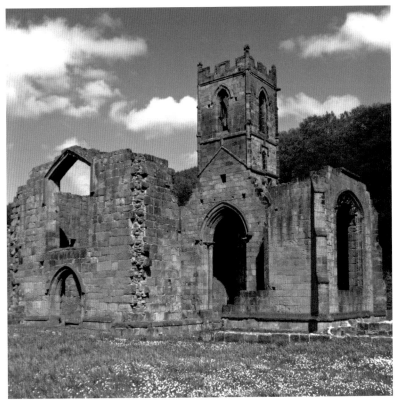

Mount Grace Priory

Places to Visit

Ampleforth Abbey & Church w

Monastic buildings dating from 1860 to the present day. Part of Roman Catholic public school. Abbey and part of gardens open to the public during daylight hours. Byroad off the B1257, 5½ miles south of Helmsley

Byland Abbey EH

Beautiful ruins, the remnant of the Rose Window being particularly inspiring.
English Heritage (charge); open April to September
Roadside 2miles west of Ampleforth

Mount Grace Priory EH/NT

☎ (01347) 868614
England's most important Carthusian ruin where monks lived and worked in individual isolated cells, one of which has been restored.
National Trust property (charge); open all year Tuesday to Sunday, 10:00am to 4:00pm (6:00pm April-September)
½ mile east of the A19 south of its junction with the A172

Mouseman Visitor Centre w

Kilburn
☎ (01347) 6218
Exhibition and sales of oak furniture made by the followers of the late Robert Thompson.

Terraced tea room overlooking views of the Kilburn White Horse. Open between Easter and end September, daily from 10:00am to 5:00pm. October to end November, Tuesday to Sunday 10:00am to 5:00pm. December, open Wednesday to Sunday 11:00am to 4:00pm
On byroad about 6miles south-east of Thirsk

National Park Centre w

Sutton Bank
☎ (01845) 597426
Information centre for the North York Moors National Park. Café and bookshop. Guided walks on advertised days and bus stop for 'Moorsbus Service'
Open all year during daylight.
Set amidst woodland roadside on the A170 at the top of Sutton Bank.

Newburgh Priory w

17th and 18th century house with many fine rooms. Wild water garden.
Private house; open to the public (charge) mid-May to end August, Wednesday only 2:00 – 5:00, also Sunday in August.

Rievaulx Abbey EH

☎ (01439) 770173
Well preserved ruins of a Cistercian monastery set in a tranquil valley surrounded by wooded hills. Advertised special events.

English Heritage property (charge); open April to end September daily 10:00am to 6:00pm
At the end of a narrow side road off the B1257 north of Helmsley.

Rievaulx Terrace Temples NT
☎ (01439) 798340
Pleasure grounds set between two mock classical temples. Delightful views of Rievaulx Abbey ruins. Special events throughout the year. National Trust (charge); open February to end of October 11:00am to 5:00pm.
On side road adjacent to the abbey lane off the B1257 north of Helmsley.

Shandy Hall w
Coxwold
☎ (01347) 6463
Medieval house, garden and museum, where Laurence Sterne author of *A Sentimental Journey* and *Tristram Shandy* lived from 1760 until his death in 1768.
Open (charge), from June to September, Wednesday and Sunday pm.

Spout House w
Restored 16th century thatched cruck dwelling restored by the NYMNPA; a one-time inn (charge).
Open Easter to October 10:00 to 4:30pm.
Roadside on B1257 about 9 miles north of Helmsley.

Recommended Walking Areas Suitable For Families
There are a number of waymarked footpaths from and guided walks from Sutton Bank National Park Information Centre.
Well placed car parks along the Hambleton Hills make suitable bases for short walks.

Off Road Cycling
Drove roads along the escarpment north of Sutton Bank offer miles of easy off-road cycling which can be linked to byways further east.

Horse Riding
Bilsdale Riding Centre at Shaken Bridge Farm, Hawnby near Helmsley YO62 5LT offer short or longer rides and instruction for beginners or the experienced.
Contact: ☎ (01439) 798225

Esk Dale & the Northern Moors

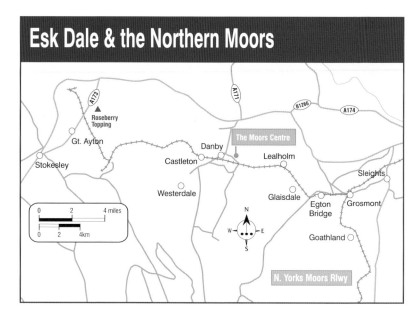

The Esk, the only truly east-flowing river, cuts a deep notch between a series of heather moors, in turn cut by remote almost hidden side valleys as the river flows on its way to the coast at Whitby. Although a railway manages to follow the river, to drive up or down the dale entails a maze of byways running to and fro along the dale. This then is a dale to be explored at leisure and by so doing find all its hidden nooks and crannies.

For some bureaucratic reason two delightful small towns were missed out of the northern edge of the national park, but that does not prevent them from being enjoyed as part of a tour around the moors. **Stokesley** to the side of the busy A172, part dormitory to Middlesbrough, still retains much of its market town atmosphere – there is a weekly produce market held every Friday and a cattle market on Tuesday. Pretty side bridges cross the River Leven where it flows through the town, and the church though restored by the Victorians, still has many recognisable features that are over 600 years old. James Cook, navigator and explorer went to school in **Great Ayton.** His school is now the Captain Cook School Museum, but if you want to see the cottage where his parents lived, you will have to go to Melbourne, Australia, for it was moved there stone by stone in 1935. Great Ayton like its neighbour, Stokesley, sits

Above: Captain Cook spent his boyhood at Great Ayton

Below: Roseberry Topping, Cleveland's 'Matterhorn'

beside the flower-decked River Leven at the foot of Easby Moor and where the 50 foot monument to Cook can be seen from miles around. There are two churches in Great Ayton, one is Victorian, but the other, All Saints, has some interesting Saxon and Norman relics. The village has a long association with the Society of Friends, or Quakers, and overlooking High Green is one of the eight Quaker schools in England; this is where the James Cook Heritage Trail starts, symbolically next to the barefoot stature of Cook in boyhood.

A little to the north is Cleveland's Matterhorn, **Roseberry Topping** whose west face was sculpted by the collapse of an ironstone mine many years ago. Anyone following the Cleveland Way usually diverts away from the main path in order to pay homage to this dominant feature; of course you can still climb the hill without going to the trouble of a long walk, there is a shorter version from the scenic car park at Gribdale Terrace near the road end east of Great Ayton.

Trains heading for the Esk Valley and Whitby must climb from Middlesbrough as far as Battersby Junction where, in order to gain height, they reverse before crossing a broad col into Kildale, and then on to Lonsdale the first of the Esk's many tributaries. In prehistoric times land on which **Kildale** village now sits was at the head of a huge lake, filling what is now the main dale, but it was the Danes who first settled here, followed by a Norman overlord who built a small wood-fenced castle on land now used by the railway station. In 1312 Friars of the Holy Cross wanted to build a monastery here but they were moved on by the Archbishop of York. It

is thought that part of the chapel they were building is now within the parish church of St Hilda.

Moving downstream we come to the moorland village of **Castleton,** at one time the largest village in Esk Dale, but now a sturdy group of stone houses built on the site of a wooden Norman fortress defended by three moats; later there was a spell of industry when local wool was woven, but the mill is now long abandoned, as was the weekly market. Two deeply-carved north-flowing side dales reach down to Castleton; the first is **Westerdale** where its namesake village sits below heather-clad grouse moors, but although its castellated hunting lodge no longer accommodates sportsmen, the village still finds employment before and after the 'Glorious Twelfth'. Over Castleton Rigg ('rigg' is the Old Norse word for ridge); the next side dale is **Danby Dale** where beneath the valley head is Botton Hall, an almost self-supporting community for the disabled run by the Camphill Trust.

Catherine Parr, sixth and surviving wife of Henry VIII, was born in **Danby.** The fourteenth century castle where she lived is now part of a farm whose walls speak of its one-time strength. It still has a vaulted dungeon and rooms where Elizabethan justices met for the Danby Court Leet and Baron; the court still administers common land and rights of way disputes. **Court Leets** are a form of local jurisdiction dating back to at least Norman times; there are four operating in the North York Moors, at Spaunton, Fyling, Whitby Laithes and Danby. The court's nominal head is known as the Lord of the Manor, but today administration is left to a legally qualified Court Steward or 'Seneschal', a title which came over with William the Conqueror.

Heather & Moorland Management

To a bystander, heather moorland may seem natural and everlasting, but this is not so. Around 5000 years ago most of what we call the moors was covered by forest. As people began to settle they cut down the trees in order to create grazing. The land then became mildly acidic, making it ideal for heather which continues to this day. Sheep still graze on the moors, but a far more important industry has grown with grouse shooting, making a significant impact on the local economy.

As both sheep and grouse live on the fresh shoots of young heather, properly managed moors cannot be left simply to their own devises and the landscape has to be carefully managed by a programme of burning old woody heather. Between October and March small patches of the moor are burned on an 8 to 15 year cycle, making a mosaic with heather at different heights. As a result and by carefully watching nesting and feeding habits, red grouse, golden plover and lapwings can breed in comfort. Without this burning, the moors would simply return to scrub woodland.

Two narrow roads climb out of Esk Dale from Castleton and nearby Danby; both are unfenced for much of the way, so motorists must keep an eye open for sheep. Stone flagged paths used by travellers in ancient times criss-crossing the surrounding moors are marked by upright stones, earthworks and pre-historic burial mounds, or 'howes' as they are called locally. Both roads reach the A171, making an easy link between the coast and Middlesbrough. Two reservoirs east and west of the watershed on Gerrick Moor are available for fishing; Scaling Dam, the largest is to the east and Lockwood in the west.

Just outside Danby a village immortalised by Canon JC Atkinson in his *Forty Years in a Moorland Parish,* **The Moors National Park Centre** at Crow Wood is within the grounds and buildings of Danby Lodge, an 18th century hunting retreat. Here you can find information about the national park from exhibitions, or enjoy a light meal in the tea rooms; signposted walks radiate from the lodge and there is a children's play area. Crow Wood with its bird hides and an electronic information screen contains remnants of the forest that once covered most of Esk Dale. On the lawn in front of the centre carefully plotted rings on the stump of a much loved copper beech which died of old age are in the process of being converted into a history tree. Standing at 981 feet above sea level at the highest point on the road up to the A171, Danby Beacon makes an excellent viewpoint for the dale and its surrounding moors. The partly flagged track of Pannierman's Causeway dates from pre-historic times, but was still used a little over a century ago by coal and fish carriers.

Above: The Moors National Park Centre, Danby Lodge

Left: The electronic information board at Danby Lodge is a popular innovation

Bridges over the Esk

Because travelling along the dale has always meant crossing and re-crossing the river, over twenty bridges follow its course. Several of the older hump-backed crossings are still in existence, but not all can carry modern traffic. From Westerdale downstream, the first bridge is **Hunter's Sty** which was restored in 1874, but is thought to date from the 13th century. Next is double-arched **Dibble Bridge** across as the name describes, a deep pool first recorded in 1301. **Duck Bridge** crosses the river below Danby Castle taking its name after the man who built it. Lower downstream, unfortunately partly dominated by the more modern road and railway bridges, is the graceful tree-shrouded span of **Beggar's Bridge** near Glaisdale. The romantic legend attached to this bridge tells of Thomas Ferries who as a youth was thought too poor to even ford the river in order to reach his beloved; but went to fight the Armada and made a fortune in London, returning in 1619 to claim his bride and build the bridge.

The National Park Authority has a leaflet called *Bridges of the Esk* that traces much of the history of these fascinating old structures.

Below: Beggar's Bridge near Glaisdale has a romantic history

The two **Fryup Dales** Great and Little have nothing to do with an indulgent breakfast, but the word comes from a combination of the Old English words *Freya* who was a Norse goddess, and *Hop*, a dale; so in other words we are looking at Freya's Dale. The two dales meet at Fairy Cross Plain, a reminder that this was once the legendary haunt of little people who, if you asked them kindly, would churn butter in the night. Quiet side roads link both dales before climbing out on to moors renowned for the juiciness of the bilberries growing there. The eastern way into great Fryup Dale once had six gates until as a stone marker states, they were removed by local donors, to *'use well time saved'*.

Coming down from the moors, whichever way you approach **Lealholm** means a steep descent, but the journey is well worth the effort. Grouped around a spacious riverside village green are attractive cottages, shops, tea-rooms and an inn; and best of all, delightful views out on to the moors, the one from Lealholm Bank being especially so. For garden enthusiasts there is Poet's Corner Shrub Nursery and what is probably the largest semi-natural rock garden in the country. Although private and only open on special occasions, the garden which follows Crunkley Gill above the village is a riot of trees, ferns and rare plants. More steep roads reach **Glaisdale,** a village built on a series of terraces across the hillside which make it an ideal base for any number of walks; many of them are along ancient paved 'trods', once the village's only link with the outside world. The path downstream through East Arncliffe Wood to Egton Bridge is particularly attractive with a 'wishing stone' along the way. It once had a tree growing from its centre round and if you walked nine times, any wish you made would come true! Odd as it may seem today, Glaisdale was for ten years from 1866 a hive of activity when ironstone was mined and there was also a thriving weaving industry during the 16th and 17th centuries.

A rarity in Esk Dale, **Egton Bridge** sits beside the river, one of the prettiest villages in North Yorkshire. Legend has it that William the Conqueror's blacksmith horrified by his master's excesses during the 'harrying of the north', deserted and settled here. It is probably the fact of this remoteness that allowed Catholicism to hold on while the rest of the country was bowing to Henry VIII's Reformation. It is the birthplace of Father Nicholas Postgate who in 1697 aged 82 was executed at York for baptising a child and who is remembered by pilgrimages to the village. A massive Catholic church dedicated to St Edda overshadows the village and half way up the hill is the house where he conducted secret masses. In a happier vein, on the first Tuesday in August the village holds a giant gooseberry show, dating back as far as 1800 with berries the size of plums on display.

Egton proper sits astride a breezy crossroads where moorland starts to give way to arable farming. Its name comes from 'Egetune', a 'town of oaks' to the first Anglo-Saxons and its inhabitants still show a great sense of character. A few years back the local authority decided to close down the public toilet in the village centre, a questionable move in a place visited by large numbers of tourists. The village tweaked the nose of officialdom by renaming itself 'Clochemerle' and won its case! *Clochemerle*, by Gabriel Chevalier is a book about village rivalry over the siting of a pissoir – there are still photographs in the pub opposite of the Egton locals dressed in French costume at the formal reopening ceremony.

Without doubt, **Grosmont** is the most visited place in Esk Dale. Two railways join here, one is the Middlesbrough to Whitby service, but it is the other the **North York Moors Railway** which brings people flocking to ride on steam hauled trains across the moors and down to Pickering. Placed at the junction of the Rivers Esk and Murk Esk, the village sits in a wooded hollow where motorists have to carefully navigate the steep inclines; one is at least 1 in 3, and up which Coast to Coast walkers must labour on the last leg of their way to Robin Hood's Bay. The name Grosmont comes from a subsidiary of the French based Grandimont Priory built in 1394, but no trace of it remains. In 1836 a rich ironstone seam was found during the building of the railway and many of the houses date from then.

Railways across the moors

Of the three railways which have served the area, only two are still in operation and one of those, albeit the most renowned, is just a fraction of its original length, but what is left makes it one of the most popular lines in the country.

Powerful steam locomotives haul trains along the scenic **North York Moors Railway** from Grosmont to Pickering, the end of a line that once ran as far as Malton. The remainder still follows the route laid down in 1836 by George Stephenson; at first trains were stage coaches on top of simple bogies, pulled along the rails by horses, then at Beck Hole near Goathland, they were hauled by rope up a 1 in 15 incline. A cause of many accidents, the problem was solved by blasting what became known as the Deviation Line which crosses Eller Beck four times in just over a mile, opening the line to through traffic by steam trains. It was during the building of this section that ironstone was discovered, leading to the development of the Teesside iron and steel industry. Beyond Goathland the track climbs to its highest point at Fen Bog where the track was laid on top of brushwood, then rapidly down through Cropton Forest and narrow Newton Dale into Pickering.

The **Esk Valley Line** runs a service linking Middlesbrough to Whitby by way of Battersby Junction where the old ironstone railway came down from the moors on a steep incline. Twin-coach diesel trains must reverse at the junction in order to climb over Kildale and into the delightful confines of Esk Dale.

(continued over-page)

What was once the most scenic coastal railway in the country followed the coast northwards from Scarborough, calling at places like Robin Hood's Bay and Whitby by crossing deep-cut rivers on high viaducts. Due to the unstable geology of the coast it required constant repair and as a result was abandoned around the time of the Beeching Axe. Since then the line with its sudden drops and diversions has been opened as a scenic trail for cyclists, horse riders and walkers.

Goathland Station

North York Moors Railway

Goathland

The **Murk Esk** flows down from the moors from Fen Bog joining the Esk at Grosmont. Within its valley scattered hamlets remote from busy roads can only be reached by careful navigation or on foot. The main habitation is around **Goathland** aka *Aidenfield* from being used as the set of TV soap *Heartbeat*. The village is a scattered grouping of cottages around a wide sheep-cropped green with shops and cafes using the Aidenfield title without spoiling the place. Its name has nothing to do with goats, but relates to the first settler, 'Goda', who came from Scandinavia around the 10th century. Straying sheep were kept in the village pound as recently as 1924 and could only be freed by payment of a fine. Goathland is the home of the Goathland Plough Stots, a sword dance team who perform at summer events.

Goathland makes an ideal base for moorland walks, such as by following the Roman Road into Wheeldale, or through wooded valleys where you will find any number of waterfalls. The best known of these is Mallyan Spout, a 70ft waterfall in a wooded dell reached by a path from Mallyan Spout Hotel opposite the church. Nelly Ayre Foss is a mile or so upstream along Wheeldale and Thomason Foss is in the main dale, a little upstream from the Beck Hole's pub.

The annual custom of planting the **Penny Hedge** in the river between Whitby and Sleights is an event dating from 1159 when three hunters drove a wild boar into the now ruined chapel below Sleights. At the time it was the home of a hermit who because he protected the animal, received a severe beating from the huntsmen. As he lay dying he imposed a penance that on the eve of Ascension Day each year they had to collect staves from the nearby forest, costing no more than one penny. They then had to set these staves in the tidal mud close to Whitby harbour, making a fence strong enough to withstand three tides, otherwise their lands would be forfeited to the abbot of Whitby Abbey.

Sleights is where the prosperous ship owners of Whitby built their homes away from smoke and stench during the height of the whaling industry, but nowadays it makes an ideal stopover between the moors and coast and where rowing boats can be hired for an hour or so on the gently flowing Esk.

Places to Visit

Captain Cook Boyhood School Museum w

Great Ayton
Small museum and schoolroom. Accessed down a side street opposite Cook's Boyhood statue in front of Society of Friends settlement in Great Ayton town centre. Open throughout the week during daylight hours.

The Moors National Park Centre and Crow Wood w

Danby Lodge
☎ (01439) 772737
Moors based activity and visitor centre. Children's adventure play area. Waymarked and guided walks, plus events throughout the year. Open during daylight hours.

Danby Castle w

Little Fryup Dale
One time home of Catherine Parr, sixth and surviving wife of Henry VIII. Private farmhouse open only on locally advertised days.

North York Moors Railway w

☎ (01751) 473535
Grosmont to Pickering by steam trains on advertised schedules.

Recommended Walking Areas Suitable for Families

Esk Valley Walks
Waymarked walks in Westerdale; along the Esk Valley; Common

Dale & Castleton and from Danby Lodge. Also from Fryup Dale towards the moors. Woodland areas are particularly special in spring when wild daffodils are in bloom.
Walk leaflets available from the Moors National Park Centre.

Off Road Cycling

There are no truly off road cycle areas except say the old track across Lealholm Moor, but the network of minor roads is suitable for comparatively traffic-free rides. The *Moor to Sea Cycle Network* follows the Esk on its way from Great Ayton to Whitby. Use the Esk Valley Line railway to make a round trip.

Horse Riding Centre

Great Fryup Dale
☎ (01947) 897470

Fishing Permits

River Esk (Egton Estates, Egton Bridge) tel: (01947 895466
Lockwood Beck Reservoir
☎ (01287) 660501
Scaling Dam ☎ (01287) 643026

Boating

Rowing boat and canoe hire at Ruswarp near Whitby.
☎ (01947) 810329

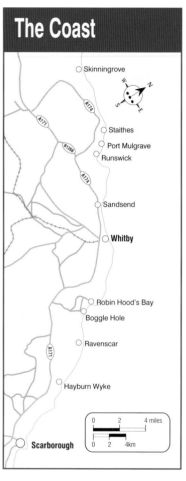

The North York Moors National Park includes the stretch of unique coastline formed by Jurassic rocks. It runs south from White Stones near Boulby, to Long Nab just a mile or so short of Scarborough. While the national park boundary starts a little to its south, the one-time ironstone mining village of **Skinningrove** near Loftus is worth visiting if only to see the Cleveland Ironstone Mining Museum. For a village devastated by loss of its main industry, the mine is once again at the centre of village life, while pit head gear and silos, the accoutrements of modern mining sit delicately within the confines of the national park at Boulby **Potash Mine,** a mile or so inland from the highest point along the coast.

Left: Kippers at Fortune's, Whitby

Below Top: Skinningrove Ironstone Mine

Below Bottom: Staithes Harbour beneath Cowbar Nab

Riches from beneath the Moors – part 2

Potash Mining

Over 5,000 ft/1,525m deep beneath the moors and several miles out under the North Sea, rich beds of potash and salt are being mined on a monumental scale. Working in conditions of high temperature and humidity, miners toil, not with pick and shovel, but with mechanical diggers loading the raw material into huge lorries which like the pit ponies of old, never see the light of day. At the end of their short working lives, corroded by salt, they are simply turned into a worked-out passage, there to remain. Mined products are brought to the surface by conveyor and shipped to the Teesside chemical industry as the raw material for fertiliser and a range of everyday chemicals.

5,000ft deep Boulby Potash Mine reaches miles out beneath the North Sea

Staithes

Turn off the A174 for **Staithes,** but don't be disappointed with your first view of the place; all its true delights are hidden way below modern housing near the village car park on the site of the coastal railway station. The road drops steeply into the old village where fishermen's cottages are set cheek by jowl mainly on the east side of the

deep ravine of Roxby Beck. Fishing boats shelter in a harbour protected by two stone breakwaters beneath Cowbar Nab. When James Cook was a boy he served as apprentice to a Staithes' draper, studying navigation in his spare time. At that time the then open harbour was prey to storms, but it still attained the rank of the largest fishing port along the coast when thousands of tons of fish competed for space with even greater tonnage of ironstone. The wide open harbour was prey to storms and many houses, including the draper's shop were washed away, but a plaque on the house replacing it commemorates Cook's stay. So crowded is the village that it boasts the narrowest street in England, Dog Loup is so narrow that only dogs and the slimmest humans can use it.

There is a small sandy beach near the eastern breakwater and the cosy Cod and Lobster pub on its landward side is famous for crab sandwiches.

Yorkshire Cobles

Staithes boats are still built to the typical design of fishing boats along the Yorkshire coast. Called 'cobles', pronounced co-bles, (two syllables), the unique design allows them to be beach launched. Clinker built, broad in the beam with high pointed prows and a small square stern, they are thought to be descended from Viking longboats. Originally powered by sail and crewed by up to five men, nowadays with the luxury of inboard engines, they only need one or two men for inshore fishing.

Hinderwell and **Port Mulgrave** are twin villages south east of Staithes. Set between the moors and coastal scenery, they once made their living from shipping around 3,000 tons of iron-ore each week from local mines. Ore reached the port by way of a mile-long tunnel now sealed for safety reasons. Hinderwell was once known as Hilderwell, from St Hilda, abbess of Whitby who escaped the pressures of the abbey by praying in solitude beside the churchyard well that gave the village its name.

Runswick Bay gives first hint of a long battle with the constant eroding of the sea cliff, an example of how the whole coast is slipping into the sea, especially after winter storms. Runswick has comparatively little interest in fishing today; most of the boats you will see are for sport and the whitewashed cottages are mainly for holidaymakers, but the crescent of golden sands is a mecca for artists and holidaymakers alike. Walk along the sands at low tide to the second of two small streams that cut deeply into the cliffs. This is **Hob Holes**, part natural, part jet mines, but now silted up, which take their name from a Yorkshire goblin who was supposed to live down by the stream. A friendly chap, he would cure any manner of children's ailments if asked nicely enough.

Windswept Goldsborough and its single pub points the way to **Kettleness;** its houses the remnant of a larger village swept away in a cliff fall during a violent storm in 1829. Two standing stones south west of Goldsborough are said to mark the grave of the giant Wade who scooped out the Hole of Horcum. Kettleness also has bogles that are said to wash their clothes in Claymoor Well. In a field above Kettleness and near the curiously named Scratch Alley, a small mound marks the site of what was once a Roman signal station, one of a line protecting the coast between Saltburn and Scarborough.

Roxby Beck Staithes

The Jurassic Coast

The coastline from Staithes to Robin Hood's Bay has become known as the Jurassic Coast from the rocks that were laid down in a warm sea about 208 to 146 million years ago. There was an explosion of life during that time, when large reptiles were dominant and the first birds appeared. The fossilised spiral shells of ammonites, some gilded with iron pyrites (fool's gold), can be found on the sea shore at low tide, especially around Kettleness or around the north end of Sandsend Beach. Quarrymen digging alum near Kettleness in the 1800s unearthed a series of spectacular fossil reptiles; ichthyosaurs and plesiosaurs alongside ammonites and belemnites came to light, the first of many discoveries that continue to this day. Several of these finds are in Whitby's Pannet Park Museum.

When fossil hunting, always keep well away from unstable cliffs and keep a watch on the tide (it is far too easy to get trapped by the incoming sea along this coast). Only collect fossils that are lying on the ground – never dig them from cliffs or solid rock. Never enter private land without first seeking permission.

Before the A174 coast road makes a steep drop to the sea front at Sandsend, it passes through **Lythe,** a village of pleasant houses and a nice inn, but its main attraction is the sturdy cliff top church just outside the village towards Sandsend. Much of the church is as it was in Saxon times. Viking grave markers thrown out during the Victorian zeal for church rebuilding have been carefully restored and are on view inside the porch. There is a tiny blacksmith's shop in the village where the custom of Firing the Stiddy (anvil), celebrates notable events in the family of the Marquis of Normanby from nearby Mulgrave Castle.

Although the fine Georgian **Mulgrave Castle** is still in private hands, the wooded ravine in which it stands is usually open on Wednesdays and weekends, but not in May. Charles Dickens once holidayed at Mulgrave and legend has it that our friend the Giant Wade and his wife Bell while they were still on speaking terms, lived at the now ruined Foss Castle deep within the woods. The woodland walk takes in a number of sites with evocative names such as Devil's Bridge, Wizard's Glen, the Waterfall and Eagle's Nest.

Two streams flow out of Mulgrave Woods down to the seashore at **Sandsend** where 2½ miles/4km of golden sand stretch all the way to Whitby. A holiday destination in its own right, but without the bustle of its neighbour, conveniently separated by an excellent cliff-top golf course and open fields. Quiet it maybe, and although it is hard to trace, Sandsend had an industrial past. During the Roman occupation, the settlement produced cement then later alum, ironstone and even jet were mined nearby, shipped out from the now fast disappearing wooden jetty at the mouth of Sandsend Beck. Until the late 1950s, the coastal railway jostled for space along the sea front, but only walkers now use its track bed.

Runswick Bay

Whitby & the South

Technically outside the national park, nevertheless Whitby makes a perfect division between sea and moors. The town fits cosily around a busy harbour at the mouth of the River Esk; it would still be recognised by Captain James Cook who sailed from Whitby to explore the Pacific. Another local navigator, William Scoresby sailed north to chart the Arctic seas; Cook discovered Australia and the other helped guide whaling ships to their quarry.

The newest part of the town spreads behind West Cliff, but elegant town houses along Saint Hilda's Terrace date from the time when the town's prosperity was based on whaling and sealing in the high arctic. Luckily the stench of boiling whale oil no more reminds us of this cruel but highly profitable trade; all that is left is a pair of whalebones overlooking the harbour beside the statue of James Cook.

Moving downhill towards the harbour by way of Skinner Street, one of those streets where you can still find truly independent and interesting shops, we come to the swing bridge that always draws its crowds watching boats pass through to the inner harbour. The old town is on the east bank of the river, a juxtaposition of narrow streets and alleys lined with buildings which seem to rise straight from high water mark. Fishing is still a major occupation, either commercial or amateur, and if you follow your nose along Church Street towards East Pier you will come to Fortune's shop, behind which is a smoke shed where herrings, 'silver darlings', become kippers. If you are looking for a wider ranging fish menu, try the Magpie Restaurant on the western quayside, the North's answer to restaurateur Rick Stein.

Come to Whitby when there is a strong north-easterly gale and watch the waves surf between the harbour's outer piers. Countless ships have been wrecked on this lee shore and none more tragic than when the Whitby lifeboat was lost with twelve of her crew on 9th February 1861 within yards of West Pier. Only one crew member survived, Henry Freeman, whose photograph by Frank M Sutcliffe is just one of the Victorian photographer's evocative studies of the town.

Climb the 199 steps of Church Stairs towards the abbey, but stop off at St Mary's Church where the sombre graveyard became the setting for the opening passages of Bram Stoker's *Dracula*. In the story Count Dracula's

---

Riches from beneath moors – part 3

Jet is a semi-precious stone related to lignite, a form of coal which is found in small pockets along the coast. When polished it gains a lustre which gained popularity in Victorian times when small workshops in Whitby employed workmen skilled at turning this dull stone into a thing of beauty. Jet is currently enjoying a degree of popularity and there are still one or two local craftsmen making attractive items of jewellery, mostly along Church Street.

coffin was washed ashore in a storm off Whitby; taking the form of a large dog he climbed the 199 steps seeking refuge in the grave of a suicide, using it as his base for nocturnal wanderings. The church's interior is unique in England – nowhere is there such a profusion of panelling and box pews from the seventeenth and eighteenth centuries, dominated by the Cholmley family pew with its great barley-sugar twist columns.

Beyond the church is Whitby's pride a joy, the Abbey of St Hilda, founded in 657. Set on a breezy hilltop the ruins left by Henry VIII's Dissolution and later shelling by a German warship during World War 1, it still inspires visitors who come to admire English Heritage's finest property on the north-east coast.

WHITBY ABBEY

St Hilda, or Hild as she was then known was a princess, daughter of the King of Northumbria who decided to build her red sandstone church on this high hilltop where it could be seen for miles in any direction. Over the centuries the abbey grew in fame and stature, inevitably coming to the attention of raiding Vikings who razed it to the ground in 867. Later it was restored and grew in the Norman-style attracting pilgrims to the tomb of St Hilda, only to be finally wrecked on the orders of Henry VIII.

How the date of Easter was decided

Before 597 Christianity in England was split between Celtic in the north and St Augustine's Roman version in the south. Unfortunately each celebrated Easter on a different day and by chance King Oswy of Northumbria adhered to the Celtic version while his wife Queen Aenfled preferred the other. To save marital harmony the question was resolved in 664 at the Synod of Whitby, since when the date of Easter has followed the rule of Rome.

Caedmon

A sandstone cross near St Mary's Church commemorates Caedmon a shy and retiring monk who rather than join his fellows preferred the company of farm animals. One night so the story goes, he dreamed that an angel asked him to sing, and when he woke he discovered he had a wonderful singing voice, which he continued to use to good effect for the rest of his life: his *Song of Creation* became the earliest known poem in English literature.

Whalebones frame the old town and Whitby Abbey

Of the museums and other tourist attractions two must be singled out as by far the best. The elegant harbourside Georgian house on Grape Lane is where James Cook stayed during his apprenticeship as a navigator and is now the **Captain Cook Memorial Museum,** a must for anyone following his amazing life story. Uphill along St Hilda's Terrace to the west of the harbour, **Pannet Park Museum** is a cornucopia of Moors and Coast memorabilia (including a macabre 'Hand of Glory'), together with items from the town's maritime past that includes a room devoted to James Cook and the Scoresby's father and son. A Jurassic Walk including a model dinosaur winds its way through geological prehistory in a freshly designed garden – a must for children.

The Captain Cook Memorial Museum is on Whitby's Grape Lane in the house where he lodged

Whitby Abbey – founded by St Hilda in 867

199 steps lead to Whitby's St Mary's Church and the Abbey

Fortune's kippers are world famous

Captain James Cook

Captain Cook's statue overlooks Whitby Harbour

The James Cook Heritage Trail follows his life story from his birthplace in 1728 at Marton near Middlesbrough; the museum in Stewart Park stands close to the site of his boyhood home. He was educated at Great Ayton where he lived with a Quaker family who were to guide him on his way to fame. Later he moved to Staithes, apprenticed to the village draper, and in his spare time became interested in navigation. His early seafaring days were spent on flat-bottomed colliers plying along England's eastern seaboard; lodging while ashore with another Quaker family whose house is on Whitby's Grape Lane. He first achieved fame by charting Canada's River St Lawrence, enabling General Wolfe storm the Heights of Abraham and capture Quebec from the French. It was a Whitby-built ship the *Endeavour* that took James Cook on his voyages of exploration around the Pacific, charting much of the Australian and New Zealand coastline.

An hour's walk and a mile or so along the coast from Whitby, **Saltwick Nab** juts out into the sea, where a jumble of sedimentary rocks made up of different strata have been worn into dramatic shapes by wave action. Beyond it the rocks of Black Nab help enclose a small bay where the surf comes in with thrilling power when the wind is from the north-east.

If when you are in **Robin Hood's Bay** and see fully booted and rucksack wearing walkers march down the steep village street and continue into the sea, don't worry they are not absolutely

mad, but are probably celebrating the end of their Coast to Coast Walk which began at St Bees on the west coast.

Known locally as simply 'The Bay', the village is steeped in maritime history, especially from when its main trade was not fishing, but smuggling. Houses literally on the edge of the sea were linked to each other by way of the cave-like exit of King's Beck beneath the Bay Hotel. Trap doors led into houses directly above the stream and at one time contraband would be passed from house to house without seeing the light of day. Called the Clovelly of the

North, the red roofed houses of the old village have steep staircases and many have a special landing window designed, so the locals say, to enable coffins leave the house without struggling down an almost vertical stairway.

Fishing is still an important part of the village economy, but without a harbour, boats must be hauled out of the sea and parked at the end of the street. At one time there were as many as 35 cobles, together with five herring boats, when the village was larger than now, but sea erosion, only stopped by the massive sea wall, engulfed a significant part. Strange rock formations called 'Scars' hereabouts, the skeleton of eroded strata, trap pools full of sea creatures, and at low tide acres of firm sand reach out to Boggle Hole where a youth hostel uses an old water mill. Fossils also abound, with fresh ones appearing after each high tide.

As befits a fishing village, crab in all its forms sits high on the menu of the two pubs in a street lined with curio shops, all in marked contrast with the more recent part of the village. This upper section developed when the railway came through, and in fact, the main car park is on the site of the station. There are a couple of hotels and a pub for those who shirk at the thought of climbing down then back along the main street, but the views are still superb.

Although **Ravenscar** is only four miles as the crow flies or the coastal walker treads from Robin Hood's Bay, it is considerably more by road. Raven Hall Hotel sits on a 600 ft/182m high breezy headland where the Romans once had a signal station, leaving an as yet un-deciphered plaque now in

Pannet Park Museum, Whitby. Terraced paths lead down to the rocky beach, and the views north towards Robin Hood's Bay make up for the lack of safe bathing.

Ravenscar – 'The Town That Never Was'

Hoping to create a new holiday resort in competition with Scarborough, during the 1890s a group of businessmen bought land at Ravenscar. Unfortunately they never looked at the major requirement for a holiday resort, namely a good beach with easy access, something which is lacking at Ravenscar. As a result there were few who were willing to make their homes on this exposed site; the streets, drains and water supply laid out in anticipation of an influx of 1500 buyers are still there, but only a forlorn scattering of houses together with an empty station square remain from the 'town that never was'.

The moors have their final eastward fling near Ravenscar and are at their best in late summer. Our forefathers knew these moors and built a whole series of mounds and dykes to the west of Stoupe Brow, but for what purpose only they knew. North from the hotel the coast makes the graceful curve of Robin Hood's Bay; in between parallel lines of eroded strata show up at low tide, but shoreward the land is unstable. This was one of the reasons why the

Above left and right: Robin Hood's Bay

coastal railway was abandoned; the trail replacing it has any number of sudden drops, making cycling along it quite exciting. Not all the slumping is natural for much of the land was quarried for alum until the late 1800s. The National Trust has an information centre where you can pick up a leaflet covering the nearby Geological Trail, or join one of the frequent guided walks.

Riches from beneath the moors – part 4

For over two hundred years, **Alum** was mined and quarried beneath the moors and along the coast, but nowhere in such quantities as at Ravenscar. This was one of Britain's earliest chemical industries and came about from King Henry VIII's quarrel with the Church of Rome. Alum a complex double sulphate of potassium and aluminium was used as a 'mordant' to fix the colour of turkey-red dyed wool and in tanning. Until the 1600s it was a papal monopoly which the king broke by sending his spies to Italy and whose reports must have raised the royal eyebrows.

Occurring as shale, the quarried alum went through a complex process involving roasting in kilns to create a powder which was leached by boiling in of all things, human urine collected from London pubs! This strange alchemy continued until the 1870s, using an egg as a simple hydrometer. Remains of the extensive buildings as well as quarries can still be traced while exploring Ravenscar's Geological Trail. When finished, alum was taken down to the beach along a still visible tramway cut from the rock and loaded on to coasters at low tide.

South of Ravenscar is **Beast Cliff** where sailors would fill their casks with fresh water from Watersplash, a cliff waterfall fed by one of a number of springs issuing between layers of clay along the unstable coastline. Although the Cleveland Way passes through, this is a little visited area that remains natural and where sloes and blackberries grow in profusion during late summer. Inland, the scattered hamlet of **Staintondale** can trace its ancestry to the first Vikings to settle in the area; road signs lead to the Shire Horse Farm where working horses are put through their paces.

At **Hayburn Wyke** a tiny bay is watered by Hayburn Beck where the Yorkshire Naturalists' Trust has a 34-acre reserve. A deep-cut water channel has exposed rocks of the Middle Jurassic layers, and the stream runs through scrub woodland before tumbling on to the rocky beach by an attractive waterfall. Nearby is Hayburn Wyke Hotel, an ideal base for a walk through the reserve. Beyond it the coast ceases to be quite so dramatic until beyond Scarborough clays and shales give way to the chalk cliffs of Flamborough Head.

Boggle Hole

Places to Visit

Captain Cook Memorial Museum w

Grape Lane, Whitby
☎ (01947) 601900
House where Cook stayed while an apprenticed seaman. Artefacts and changing exhibitions of his life and times.
Open daily: April to end October 9:45 – 5:00

Cleveland Ironstone Mining Museum w

Skinningrove
☎ (01287) 642877
Based on extensive ironstone mine it provides a fascinating part underground experience of this once major industry.

Dracula Experience w

9 Marine Parade, Whitby
☎ (01947) 601923
'Haunted' tour through the Dracula story, with animated and electronic effects.
Open daily throughout the holiday season.

Jet workshops w

Church Street, Whitby
Watch the dull stone being turned into shining jewellery.

Jurassic Garden and Park

Whitby Museum, Pannet Park, St Hilda's Terrace, Whitby
☎ (01947) 602908
Short walk tracing layers of rocks and fossils laid down in the Jurassic Period, includes life sized replica of the Jurassic crocodile fossil inside the museum.
Open daylight hours

Pannet Park Museum w

St Hilda's Terrace, Whitby
☎ (01947) 602908
Fascinating collection of local memorabilia, including fossils, a 'hand of glory', carved jet, model sailing ships and links with Captain Cook's and the Scoresbys' exploits.
Open: Tuesday to Sunday (plus Bank Holiday Mondays) 9:30-4:30

Robin Hood's Bay

The Clovelly of the north. Ancient fishing village at the foot of its steep main street lined with curio shops and two pubs.

Ravenscar Geological Trail. - NT

Self guided trail through the site of alum production between the 1600s and 1870.
Nearby pattern of streets without houses are from a failed scheme to create a resort rivalling Scarborough.

St Mary's Church w

Whitby
Parish church adjacent to Whitby Abbey. Interesting box pews and 'barley sugar' pillars. Reached by 199 steps from quayside, or abbey car park. Open daily.

St Oswald's Church w

Lythe
Saxon Church with restored Viking grave markers. Open daily throughout the summer.

Skinner Street

Whitby
The town's premier shopping street.

Staintondale Shire Horse Farm

Working horses, smithy and stables – the farm is signposted along the narrow lane south of Ravenscar.
Open: Sunday, Tuesday, Wednesday and Friday 10:30 – 4:30

The Whitby Tour w

☎ 0191) 5170417
Hop on and off open topped bus tour between Whitby and the abbey. Operates April to end September 10:00 – 4:55

Whitby Abbey – EH

Evocative ruins founded by St Hilda in 680 high above Whitby's East Shore. Reached from abbey car park or by the 199 steps from the quayside.
Open: 1 April – end September,10:00 – 6:00 October, 10:00 – 5:00. 1 November – end March, 10:00 – 4:00

Whitby Wizard Experience w

The Crescent, Whitby
☎ (01947) 810470
Hands on science with a light-heated slant. Open daily throughout the year.

Recommended Walking Areas Suitable for Families

☎ (08712) 002233
Arriva's frequent service, 93 & X93, runs along the coast from Middlesbrough, through Whitby and Robin Hood's Bay (93 only), to Scarborough.
By using this service any number of linear short or long walks can be followed along the coastal paths.

Mulgrave Woods are open Wednesdays and Weekends throughout the year except in May.

Walks around Ravenscar led by National Trust Rangers.

Off Road Cycling

Most of the old coastal railway trail is open to cyclists, walkers and horse riders.

Horse Riding

Off road riding offered by stables at:
Robin Hood's Bay. ☎ (01947) 000249
Staithes ☎ (01947) 840134
n.b. Beach riding is not permitted except at Upgang ravine, Sandsend

Sea Fishing and sails

Short sails and longer fishing trips are on offer by a number of boat companies, including a 40% scale version of Captain Cook's Endeavour. Find them along Whitby's quayside. Rowing boats and canoes can be hired on the Esk at Ruswarp upstream of Whitby.

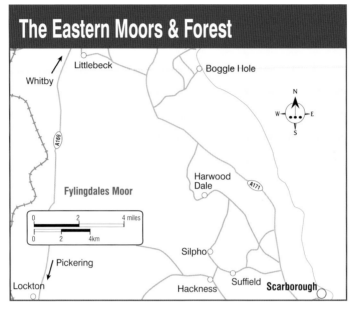

The Eastern Moors & Forest

The moors of this section are conveniently bounded by two main roads, the A171 and A169. In the north, open moorland predominates, while to the south mature pine forests cloak deep mysterious valleys, the haunt of often rare wildlife.

Perversely we start by looking at the aptly named **Littlebeck Valley** which, although draining into the Esk, can only be reached by narrow side roads from those running north-south. Here is one of the secret places on the moors: part woodland and so well hidden it can only be explored on foot from one of three car parks. **Littlebeck** village at the bottom of two steep and narrow lanes from the B1416 is where the August Rose Queen is bizarrely floated down the river on a raft. A path from the village wanders upstream through ancient woodland, past a hollowed boulder known as the Hermitage where around 20 people can sit in comfort; and little further on the track leads to **Falling Foss**. This 40ft/12m waterfall in a sylvan setting is close to Midge Hall Tea Rooms, a truly unexpected find. Beyond it the path leads to **May Beck** picnic site, the base for even more forest walks or maybe a waiting car, but with energy to spare it is possible to make a round trip by following paths to the west of the valley.

Fylingdales Moor

Nowadays something of an anachronism post-Cold War, the science-fiction radar-housing of a truncated pyramid which replaced the giant golf balls on **Fylingdales Moor,** hopefully waits in vain for nuclear missiles. Still guiding travellers, the moor's summit ridge is lined with ancient crosses south-eastwards from Whinstone Ridge above May Beck where an outcrop, or 'cill', of basalt forms a straight line across the moor. How many more stones are hidden beneath the peat can only be guessed, but an accidental roadside fire in 2003 uncovered over 190 rocks decorated with strange markings. Beyond Eller Beck and opposite the radar station, the North York Moors Railway's summit crosses Fen Bog where a nature reserve looks after a rare habitat based on a 38 foot deep bog.

Lilla Howe Cross

A little to the north-east of the Ministry of Defence boundary on Fylingdales Moor, Lilla Howe Cross stands on top of an earth mound at the junction of four moorland tracks. An important waymark since early times, it is supposed to mark the grave of Lilla, faithful servant of King Edwin of Northumbria, who gave his life in 626 by intercepting an assassin's dagger meant for the king.

Dalby & Langdale Forests

South of Fylingdales Moor, two vast intermingled forests stretch unbroken across deeply indented narrow dales, running almost unbroken towards the Vale of Pickering.

While Langdale Forest is not quite as open for recreation as its neighbour, it does have a number of accessible attractions. In particular the village of **Harwood Dale** makes a good starting point for drives and cycle rides, together with forest walks from the scenic viewpoint on **Reasty Bank.** When driving to Harwood Dale from the Scarborough road, look out for the side turning as it easily missed amongst the dense trees.

Close to the forest edge near the high point of the A171 before it drops down to Scarborough is **Standing Stones Rigg,** where a vast number of ancient stones have been discovered over the years, including a 32ft/9.7m diameter circle of twenty-one stones, making it one of the most important archaeological sites on the moors.

The River Derwent forms a division between the two forests. Fed by tributaries with evocative names like Whisper Dales and Trout's Dale, they are crying out to be explored, but only on foot, or mountain bike. Above Whisper Dales, the neighbouring hamlets of **Silpho** and **Suffield** are home to farmers taking advantage of the rich limestone soil on the flat-topped eastern outliers of the Tabular Hills. A short two-mile forest trail from Silpho passes a Bronze Age burial mound. However, if you want something more ambitious, why not try the 16mile/26km Reasty Bank to Allerston Forest Walking Trail? As it is not circular, careful planning is needed, ideally with a car at each end of the walk. Forestry Commission leaflets for both walks are available at the Visitor Centre at Low Dalby.

Rustic **Hackness** fills a tranquil sunny corner where Whisperdales Beck joins the Derwent. It was first settled in 680 by a group of breakaway nuns from St Hilda's Abbey in Whitby, but now there is a fine Georgian manor house belonging to Lord Derwent, and a Norman church with a preaching cross dating from the eighth century. Across the road from the church a little stream flows along a shallow channel beneath a high stone wall, a popular place where children can float twigs.

Following the Derwent downstream, the road enters the narrow wooded confines of **Forge Valley**. A National Nature Reserve, Forge Valley gets its name from a long-gone iron smelter that used charcoal made from the surrounding woodlands. Trees have now returned to the dale, thriving above woodland flowers on the lime-rich soil. It is this limestone which causes the Derwent to shrink to a mere trickle in places, by disappearing into sink holes, and filling a natural aquifer beneath the Vale of Pickering. Nature and geological trails and bird watching sites help visitors appreciate the valley; along with interpretive boards which you can find in roadside and main car parks.

How the River Derwent changed direction

The Ordnance Survey map appears to show a wide valley running towards the sea from Hackness, but surely the Derwent flows south through Forge Valley into the Vale of Pickering? Until the last Ice Age the river certainly flowed east, but catastrophic flooding as the land warmed was blocked by ice still filling what became the North Sea. The resulting floodwater carved a channel through the narrow valley and out into what became Lake Pickering. Eventually a natural dam in the west, below Whitewell-on-the-Hill on the A64 beyond Malton, burst allowing the river to follow its new course, down to the Humber,

As the lake slowly drained it left behind some of the richest agricultural land in the country, but unfortunately and until the early 1800s regular flooding made farming difficult. An answer came when a local entrepreneur Sir George Cayley, built levees along the Derwent and, more important, dug the Sea Cut, an overflow canal along the original course of the river, taking floodwater away from the vale.

Quiet byways and a forest drive (toll), wind their way through the mature woodlands of Dalby Forest. Over in **Staindale** a side road drops down from the minor road above Thornton-le-Dale, where the visitor centre at Low Dalby makes a perfect place to learn all there is about the forest's story and its wildlife. Short waymarked walks will offer a satisfying alternative before continuing along the Forest Drive. Picnic sites together with forest walks in High Staindale or near the Bickley Gate exit have enough scope for several days exploration.

The Moorcock Inn at **Langdale End** takes a bit of finding; you reach it from the Bickley Gate, but the search is well worth the effort. The pub is a rare still in use example of a traditional 'long house' where humans and animals once shared the same roof. The locals call Langdale, 'Little Switzerland', go there and you will see why.

Places to Visit

w = suitable in wet weather
NT = National Trust
EH = English Heritage

Dalby Visitor Centre & Forest Drives w

Staindale – accessed from the A169 about 3 miles from Pickering.
☎ (01751) 60295
An ideal place to learn about and begin to explore the local forests.

Walking trails, cycling routes, together with an orienteering course at Dixon's Hollow; 'Go Ape!' the woodland adventure course is close by.
Open during daylight hours

(continued over page)

Above: Hackness counts time in centuries of tranquillity

Right: Forge Valley Nature Reserve

Places to Visit

Scarborough w

(Just a small sample of the attractions available)
Scarborough Castle (EH)
☎ (01723) 372451
Open: April - end September 10:00 – 5:00 October – end March !0:00 – 5:00 (4:00 winter months)
Sir Alan Ayckbourn plays at the Stephen Joseph Theatre. Enquiries ☎ (01723) 370541
North Bay Railway – working scale versions of classic locomotives in Northstead Manor Gardens.
☎ (01723) 368791
Sea Life and Marine Sanctuary.
☎ (0871) 4232110

Recommended Walking Areas Suitable for Families

Littlebeck and Old May Beck Forest Walks

Reasty Bank forest Trail
Waymarked trails from scenic car parks throughout Dalby Forest

Off Road Cycling Areas

Cycling trails of varying standards throughout Dalby Forest, especially from Dixon's Hollow. Bike Hire can be found at Purple Mountain Bike Centre, Dalby Courtyard. ☎ (01751) 460011. Trail maps available at the bike centre or visitor centre.

Whinstone Ridgeway across Fylingdales Moor.

Horse Riding

Bridleways through Whisperdales; High & Low Dales; Beacon Brow; Broxa & Dalby Forests.

6. SOUTH OF THE MOORS – TOWNS ALONG THE A170

Below: Helmsley Castle

South of the moors

The First Settlers

Around 10,000 years ago, the forerunners of towns and villages lining the A170, Scarborough to Thirsk road would have had a stunning view of a tranquil lake. The now long vanished Lake Pickering, for that is what it was before it drained to form the fertile vale, was the result of a massive build-up of glacial melt-water at the end of the last ice age. These early Yorkshire men and women lived in timber and thatch round houses, usually on stilts rising from the lake's margins. One of these buildings together with a range of artefacts has recently been discovered by archaeologists who are of the opinion that it is one of Britain's earliest permanent habitations.

Due to its regular flooding, but needing to be close to the fertile land of the Vale of Pickering, a line of almost equidistant settlements grew along a track that became the A170. Starting from the east, after leaving Scarborough we come to the twin villages of **East** and **West Ayton**, kept apart by the infant River Derwent where it leaves the narrow confines of Forge Valley. Both are residential outliers of Scarborough, but the western half is the oldest, a feature acknowledged by the boundary of the national park which dissects the two. In West Ayton the remains of a fourteenth-century castle stand guard over the entrance to Derwent Dale, but many of its stones were plundered in 1775 to build a bridge connecting the two villages.

Moving west, the group of mellow stone houses of **Wykeham** surround a church with a unique lych gate built in the form of a tower. Local legend has it that it was the result of a quarrel between two sisters who though wanting to jointly build a church, fell out in the early stages of its construction; one built a tower, but the other erected the main church building a discrete distance away. The truth however, is that the tower later cut by its lych gate is all that remains of a Cistercian nunnery built in 1153. More recent **Wykeham Abbey** is set amidst glorious parkland south of the village, where its owner Viscount Downe occasionally opens it to visitors.

It was a Yorkshireman who first took to the air

A road sign on the outskirts of **Brompton** proudly announces that it is the birthplace of manned flight. Long before the Wright brothers took to the air at Kitty Hawk, Squire Sir George Cayley of Brompton Hall devised an aircraft to fly one of his coachmen 50yds across Brompton Dale in 1853. It is hardly surprising to note that the intrepid aviator on climbing from the inevitable wreckage promptly handed in his notice.

Sir George Cayley was an inventive man, not only was this the first recorded flight by a manned aircraft, but he had successfully built small gliders as long ago as 1804. Another and far more useful innovation to farmers was the opening of the Sea Cut above Forge Valley, taking flood waters away from the Vale of Pickering. Small though it may be, alongside Sir George's inventions, Brompton has a long history; there was once a castle, the hunting residence of Kings of Northumbria and its church gained a mention in the Domesday Book. It was in this church on 4th October 1802, that the poet William Wordsworth married locally born Mary Hutchinson. If you want to explore further afield from the village, try the drive north into **Wykeham Forest** where there is a short trail from a scenic picnic site.

Oddly for despite there being some very attractive countryside nearby, the national park boundary takes a wide sweep north above **Ebberston** where its eighteenth century hall, open on advertised days, is probably the smallest stately home in the country; only three bays wide and one storey high, it is set amongst attractive water gardens. A folk legend speaks of the battle fought near Ebberston in the 7th century, between King Aldfrith of Northumbria and his father King Oswy: wounded in the battle, Aldfrith hid in a nearby cave since known as Alfred's. The battle is said to have taken place around the pre-historic earthworks of Scamridge Dykes where there is a viewpoint and a picnic site on the edge of Dalby Forest.

The national park very firmly claims **Thornton–le–Dale** within its control. As far back as 1907 it was voted the most beautiful village in Yorkshire, an accolade most people who stop there will happily concur. Despite having to straddle the A170, it manages to retain an atmosphere from a less frenetic age; from the twelve almshouses built in 1670 by Lady Lumley and still in use today, to maybe the 600 year old market cross together with a pair of stocks. Eschewing too many of the type of adornments that can spoil an attractive place, the village seems to have just the right number of shops, cafes and inns to satisfy most visitor's needs – there is even a vintage car showroom on the western edge of the village that should please most 'petrol heads'.

The village car park is handily near the centre, next to a pond with hungry ducks. Across the main road and beyond the alms houses and then along a side path following Thornton Beck, is one of the most photographed cottages in the north. The delightfully propor-

tioned thatched cottage fronted by a colourful garden has featured in any number of calendars, magazine covers and chocolate boxes. Nearby stands the parish church with the grave of one Matthew Grimes who died in 1875 aged 96. He stood guard over Napoleon on St Helena until the latter's death when he helped carry the coffin.

Sat across the junction of two busy roads, **Pickering** justifiably claims the title of 'Gateway to the Moors'. Due to its position very early on it became an important market town for the surrounding area and a castle was built in the twelfth century to control movement between the moors and places beyond the Vale of Pickering. The castle now maintained by English Heritage, was used by medieval kings as a hunting lodge; in fact some parts of the old Royal Forest of Pickering are still owned by Her Majesty the Queen. Not every king had happy memories of their stay here; Richard II was murdered at Pontefract soon after leaving Pickering and Edward II had to use its shelter following his trouncing by the Scots at the Battle of Byland Abbey in October 1322.

Modern Pickering is an attractive place, especially in spring when it is alive with flowers. There is a regular Monday market when farmers come in from the nearby dales and moors to buy and sell and meet their friends. As befits a busy market town, there is an excellent range of shops, pubs and hotels, such as the two swan hotels, one black and the other white and the Forest and Vale, to name just three, all renowned

Thornton-le-Dale is considered to be the most beautiful village in Yorkshire

for their good food and cheerful banter on market days.

Pickering's Parish Church

St Peter and St Paul's church is famous for its fifteenth century murals, each depicting a biblical scene, or legends such as St George slaying the dragon. Considered idolatry and covered with whitewash by the Puritans and then again by a Victorian parson after their discovery in 1851, they were eventually rediscovered in 1878 and restored to their former glory.

Beck Isle Museum of Rural Life stands beside Pickering Beck, housing items of local interest such as a farmhouse kitchen, a barber's shop and a Victorian bar in what was originally a college of agriculture. Nearby is Beckside Craft Centre where local artisans sell their wares. Pickering has its own theatre, the Kirk, in what was once a Methodist chapel and where a varied programme is staged throughout the year. And for anglers, there is the trout farm beyond the railway station, where specially bred fish seem to queue to be caught, so much so that there is a restriction on the number caught.

The North York Moors Railway's Southern Terminus

Steaming along narrow wooded Newton Dale, a regular service of steam trains runs from the station in Pickering town centre, over the moors by way of Goathland to Grosmount in Esk Dale where it joins the Middlesbrough to Whitby service. Pickering is also the headquarters of the railway society which is mainly run by volunteers.

Pleasantly located half way between Pickering and Helmsley, with the A170 skirting to its south, **Kirkbymoorside** has existed since before the Domesday Survey. This Church by the Moors, or 'Kirby' as the locals call it, makes a useful base for exploring the southern moors. There is a busy market each Wednesday and along with a good range of shops, pubs and restaurants, the town also has a thriving community hall where shows of every description from art to flower and vegetable displays are staged throughout the year – there are even brass band performances. Cairns and mounds dot the nearby moors, but there is little evidence of Kirby's long history; two castles have long since disappeared apart from stones from one of them that were used to build a tollbooth in the town centre. Even the church hides its Norman foundations since it was restored during the Victorian zeal

Pickering Castle

79

for such things.

George Villiers, the 2nd Duke of Buckingham (1628-1687), was Kirby's most notorious resident, albeit temporarily. Once a dazzlingly wealthy courtier and friend of King Charles II, he died from drink, penniless in the home of one of his tenants. His burial was as odd as his life with his intestines interred at Helmsley and the rest of him in Westminster Abbey. Parish records described him as 'George Vilaus, lord dook of bookingham'.

Slingsby Aviation

A latter day and more successful version of George Cayley's attempts at flight can be found down a quiet lane south of Kirkbymoorside. Slingsby Aviation, probably one of the last things one would expect to find around the North York Moors, manufacture military training aircraft, along with gliders and custom-made airplanes.

The main road skirts the bottom of **Kirkdale** in order to avoid a steep descent into the dale. However, an earlier version still runs down to a little wayside car park, from which a side path leads into woodland surrounding **St Gregory's Minster**. It is here that Orm Gamalsson erected a sundial to show the eight hours of the Saxon day. Not only is it an interesting relic of those times, but being written in Early English by the son of a Viking settler, it shows how rapidly immigrants were assimilated into the language and customs of their adopted country.

A Hyena's Den

Not far downstream and a little above the Minster, **Kirkdale Cave**, more a hollow than cave, was once a hyena's den. In 1821 a workman discovered a pile of bones, but rather than throw them away, took some of them to a local doctor who immediately recognised their importance. What the man had discovered were the bones of varieties of rhinoceros, bison, mammoths and lions, all of which lived in the semi-tropical climate prevalent in the area 70,000 years ago.

Even though the North York Moors National Park Authority has its head-quarters in **Helmsley**, for some reason the park boundary by following the A170 manages to slice the town in half. A picturesque town beside the River Rye and at the centre of moorland and valley roads, it holds a market on Fridays when, if you are lucky, you can find an odd corner in one of its many pubs and cafes. It was the Normans who recorded the town as *Elmslac* and built the castle that fits quietly into a backwater of the town. With its unique 'D' shaped keep, the castle led an uneventful life until the Civil War when Parliamentary troops under the command of Sir Thomas Fairfax, on capturing it, rendered it uninhabitable, much as it looks today. A walled garden associated with the castle is gradually being restored to its former glory; stately **Duncombe Park** designed by the famous architect around the time he built Castle Howard is an easy stroll away from the town.

Places to Visit

Beck Isle Museum w

☎ (01751) 476637
Pickering town centre. Collection of
local items. Open all week in summer

Castle Howard EH w

☎ (01653) 648444
South west of Malton
Vanbrugh designed seat of the Howard
family. .
Open: Mid Feb – early November,
10:00 – 4:30

Duncombe Park EH

☎ (01439) 770213
Outskirts of Helmsley
Magnificent parkland and house
surrounded by formal gardens.
Open daylight hours

Ebberston Hall w

Thornton-le-Dale
Smallest stately home in the country
set in attractive gardens.
Open: Easter to end September

Eden Camp w

☎ (01653) 697777
Beside A64, Malton
Inter-active World War II museum set in
an ex POW camp.
Open mid January – Xmas Eve, 10:00
– 5:00

Flamingoland

☎ (016538) 6287
Zoo at Kirby Misperton; 1½ miles from
A169 Pickering to Malton road.
Open daily Easter - October

North York Moors Railway w

☎ (01751) 72508
Pickering town centre
Regular steam trains to Grosmont in

Esk Dale

Nunnington Hall NT w

☎ (01439) 748283
Georgian manor house and walled
garden beside the River Rye south of
Helmsley.
Open February to October – Tuesday
to Sunday 11:00 – 5:00.Saturday and
Sunday only during early November to
mid December.

Pickering Castle (EH)

☎ (01751) 474989
Outskirts of Pickering
Well preserved motte and bailey castle.
Open daily all year Wednesday to
Sunday except Christmas and New
Year. 10:00 – 5:00

St Gregory's Minster w

Kirkdale off A170 south west of
Kirkbymoorside
Tiny Saxon church with historic
sundial.
Open daylight hours

Recommended walking areas suitable for families

Waymarked walking trails lead from
scenic picnic sites at:

Forge Valley nature Reserve
Scamridge Dyke
Woodland walks around Kirkdale

Fishing

Stocked ponds near Pickering railway
station

Golf Driving Range

Ebberston

Above and below: Helmsley Castle

Above: Helmsley village

Below: Nunnington Hall, a National Trust property

FACT FILE

Accommodation

With two major holiday destinations close to the national park's eastern border, there is a wide range of places to stay, both on the coast and further inland in one of the moorland towns and villages. At the top of the scale, hotels such as the Black Swan in Helmsley which still manages to maintain standards of hospitality that were founded in the days when it was a major stop-over for mail coaches to York and London. There are family run pubs such as the Horseshoe in Levisham offering comfortable beds a mere stroll from a friendly dining room; bed and breakfast accommodation can be found almost anywhere across the moors and coast. Self catering in cottages where you can be as relaxed as you would be at home can be used by couples up to the largest family or social group: whatever you choose simply depends on your personal preference. On top of these possibilities there are numerous listed camping and caravan sites both near the moors and along the coast.

Details of accommodation on offer can usually be found in one of the publications from the main holiday towns, or the national park authority:

North York Moors National Park Authority
The Old Vicarage
Bondgate
Helmsley
York YO62 5BP
☎ (01439) 770657
www.visitthemoors.co.uk

Yorkshire Moors and Coast Tourism Partnership
☎ (01845) 523877
www.yorkshiremoorsandcaoast.com

Yorkshire Coast Tourism Association
www.scarborough-whitby-filey.co.uk

Recreation

The North York Moors is an area catering for all levels of recreation, be it cycling, sailing or hard long distance walking, or simply sitting back and admiring the view. There are miles of cycleways and ancient trackways, some of them lined with flag stones from the days when pack horses carried goods to and fro across the moors; from fish and even contraband making their way to inland markets, to salt that ancient preservative, and iron stone wending their way to the coast or to the rapidly growing industries on Teesside.

Walking

For the hard walking devotees there are at least four long distance walks across the moors:

Cleveland Way – 177 mile circuit of the moors and coast from Helmsley to Filey Brigg.

Coast to Coast – 190 mile walk from St Bees on the Irish Sea to Robin Hood's Bay.

Lyke Wake Walk – 40 mile crossing of the moors from Osmotherley to Ravenscar

The Link Through the Tabular Hills – 48 mile trek across the southern moors linking both ends of the Cleveland Way

The national park authority has produced a series of leaflets covering waymarked walks on the moors and along the valleys. They are obtainable for a small fee of around 50p each from local shops, or from the national park headquarters; see address as above.

Cycling

Up to date details of off road cycling areas, the Moor to Sea Cycle Network and the coastal railway trail can be obtained from the national park website website.
www.visitthemoors.com

Cycle Hire:

Abbey Bike Hire, Rosedale Abbey
☎ (01751) 417095 or 417475

Purple Mountain, Dalby – Pickering
☎ (01751) 460011

Trailways, The Old Station, Hawkser, Whitby
☎ (01947) 820207
www.trailways.info

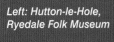

Left: Hutton-le-Hole,
Ryedale Folk Museum

Right: Helmsley Castle

Below: A view of Robin
Hoods Bay

Gliding & Microlight

Yorkshire Gliding Club, Sutton Bank ☎ (01845) 597237

Horse Riding

Please note that local bylaws do not allow horse riding on the main holiday beaches, except Upgang Ravine near Sandsend.

Riding schools are at:
Bilsdale, Hawnby ☎ (01439) 798225
Boltby ☎ (01845) 537392
Borrowby Equestrian Centre, Staithes ☎ (01947) 840134
Irton Riding Centre, Scarborough ☎ (01723) 863466
Snainton riding Centre ☎ (1723) 859218
Farsyde Riding Centre, Robin Hood's Bay ☎ (01947) 880249
Great Fryup Dale ☎ (01947) 897470
Helmsley – ☎ (01439) 770355
Hollin Hall Ride & Drive Centre, Great Fryup Dale ☎ (01947) 897470
Saltburn ☎ (01287) 622157
Sinnington ☎ (01751) 432758
Snainton ☎ (01723) 859218
Staintondale ☎ (01723) 871846

Golf Courses

Ampleforth College – 9 Hole ☎ (01904) 76881
www.ampleforthgolf.co.uk
Easingwold – 18 Hole ☎ (01347) 822474
www.huntleyhall.co.uk
Kirkbymoorside – 18 Hole ☎ (01751) 430402
www.kirkbymoorsidegolf.co.uk
Raven Hall Hotel, Ravenscar – 9 Hole ☎ (01723) 870353
www.ravenhall.co.uk
Ruswarp – 9 Hole ☎ (01947) 820550
Scarborough North Cliff – 18 Hole ☎ (01723) 355397
Scarborough Scalby Mills Road – 9 Hole ☎ (01723) 383636
Scarborough South Cliff – 18 Hole ☎ (01723) 360522

Thirsk & Northallerton – 18 hole ☎ (01845) 525115
Whitby – 18 Hole ☎ (01947) 600660

Fishing

Freshwater permits available from:

Yorkshire Water Authority ☎ (01723) 66655
Rivers Rye & Seph – (Hawnby area) ☎ (01434) 96202
               (Nunnington) ☎ (0143) 95202
River Seven ☎ (01 751) 31051
River Derwent – (Low Marishes) ☎ (01653) 693208
River Esk – (Danby) ☎ (01947) 60218
        (Ruswarp) ☎ (01947) 604658
        (Egton Bridge) ☎ (01947) 895466

Lakes & Reservoirs

Lockwood Beck Reservoir ☎ (01287) 660501
Low Osgoodby ☎ (01845) 597601
Pickering Trout Lake ☎ (01751) 47219
Hazelhead, Pickering ☎ (01751) 460215
Scaling Dam ☎ (01287) 643026
Wykeham Lakes, Scarborough ☎ 0794653001

Sea Angling

Numerous boats plying for half and full day sea trips advertise from the quayside at Whitby. All usually provide tackle and bait and refreshments. Check around to find the skipper who knows the best fishing areas.
Pier angling is permitted, but take extra care when the sea is rough, especially when accompanied by young children.

Watersports

Dinghy Sailing & Windsurfing – Wykeham Lakes ☎ 08454 560164
Rowing & Canoeing - Ruswarp, River Esk ☎ (01947) 604658
Surf Hire & Surf School – Scarborough ☎ (01723) 585585

Sports & Leisure Centres

Ampleforth College ☎ (01439) 766740
www.northyorkmoors.org.uk/sports-centres

North Ryedale, Pickering
www.nortyorkmoors-stay.co.uk

Swimming Pools

Ampleforth ☎ (01439) 766740
Guisborough ☎ (01287) 633311
Loftus ☎ (01287) 642020
Malton ☎ (01653) 693407
Pickering ☎ (01751) 473351
Scarborough ☎ (01723) 367137
Stokesley ☎ (01642) 711140
Thirsk ☎ (01845) 522447
Whitby ☎ (01947) 604640

Adventure Centres

Carlton Lodge Outdoor Centre: parties of 12 and over ☎ (01845) 522145
East Barnby Outdoor Education Centre, Whitby: adults and families weekends, parties during the week ☎ (01947) 89333
Go Ape! Dalby Forest: high wire forest adventure ☎ 0845 6432041

Bus Travel

Arriva Service (Middlesbrough – Scarborough via Whitby)
☎ (01723) 383637

Moorsbus ☎ (01845) 597000, or National Park visitor centres. Operates Sundays and Bank Holidays from April to October.

Tourist Information Centres

North York Moors Information Centres:

Sutton Bank National Park Centre ☎ (01845) 597426
The Moors National Park Centre, Danby ☎ (01439) 7772737

There are summer opening information offices at:

Dalby Forest
Hutton-le-Hole (Ryedale Folk Museum)
Ravenscar National Trust Coastal Centre
Robin Hood's Bay: Old coastguard Station
Whitby

Information points (unmanned) at:

Goathland
Grosmont
Osmotherley
Staithes
Thornton-le-Dale

Internet

Visit the North York Moors National Park Website
www.visitthemoors.co.uk.
Click – 'Discover the Place' to see an interactive map of the park.

Railways

Middlesbrough to Whitby Esk Valley Line. Check the current timetable on
National Rail Enquiries ☎ 0845 784950, or www.nationalrailways.co.uk/en/
s/timetable/times
North York Moors Railway (Moorsrail), 'Pickering Station ☎ (01751) 472508
and ☎ (01751) 473535 – Talking timetable.

Events

Details of the wide range of events, including village shows planned for
almost every month throughout the year, can be found on the national park
website:
www.visitthemoors.com

Markets on and around the moors

Bedale – Tuesday
Malton – Saturday
Pickering – Monday
Scarborough – Every day except Sunday
Stokesley – Friday
Thirsk – Monday & Saturday
Whitby – Tuesday & Saturday

Farmers' Markets

Malton – Last Saturday in the month (except August & December)
Pickering – 1st Thursday in every month

Whitby – Every Thursday (March to September)
Wykeham, Scarborough – Every Friday

How to get there

Ferry – North Sea Ferries from Rotterdam and Zeebrugge to Hull
Airports – Teesside or Robin Hood Airport, Doncaster

Rail – Mainline services via York or Middlesbrough, then onward to Scarborough or via the Esk Valley line to Whitby

By Road – Driving from the south for places to the north of the moors, take the A1(M) to Junction 49 (Dishforth), and join the A168 to Thirsk, then A19 to Ingleby Arncliffe for the A172 to Guisborough and the A171 to Whitby.
For places in the south of the moors, take the A64 via York by-pass to Malton and the A169 to Pickering, 'Gateway to the Moors'.

Coach & Bus – National Express Travel Enquiries ☎ (08717) 818181
www.nationalexpress.com

Weather

As with all high ground anyone venturing out on to the moors must be prepared and equipped for sudden changes in the weather. While this is not so much a problem in summer, the moors can have more than their fair share of snow in winter, often from sudden and unexpected storms, bringing deep road-blocking snow.
Due to its east facing aspect on the North Sea coast, the area is prone to mists (known locally as 'sea frets'), which fortunately only reach a mile or so inland. While holiday makers are shivering on the beach at Whitby, moorland walkers can often be enjoying warm sunshine within a half hour's drive from the coast.

Met office Weather Forecasts

☎ (09068) 505318 (Premium Rate Number); www.metoffice.gov.uk

Index

Index

Published in the UK by:
Horizon Editions Ltd,
Trading as The Horizon Press
The Oaks, Moor Farm Road West, Ashbourne, DE6 1HD
Tel: (01335) 347349
E-mail: books@thehorizonpress.co.uk

1st Edition

ISBN 978-1-84306-518-0

British Library Cataloguing in Publication Data:
A catalogue record for this book is available from the British Library

Printed by: Gomer Press Ltd, Llandysul, Wales
Cartography: Mark Titterton
Design: Mark Titterton

Front cover: Robin Hood's Bay (Lindsey Porter)
Back Cover top: Grosmont Station (Lindsey Porter)
Back Cover bottom: Rievaulx Abbey (Brian Spencer)

Picture Credits:
Photos are by the author except pp2, 17, 39, 50, 51, 55(top), 67 79 82 83(top), 86-7 (bottom); all taken by Lindsey Porter

---

DISCLAIMER

While every care has been taken to ensure that the information in this guide is as accurate as possible at the time of publication, the publisher and author accept no responsibility for any loss, injury or inconvenience sustained by anyone using this book.